Kinesiology

Exercise & Fitness

By Professor James Sims

Measurements & Assessments

Strength & Conditioning

Anatomy/Physiology

Human Body Movement

Sports & Exercise

Biomechanics

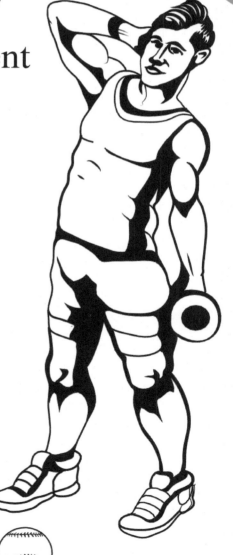

COPYRIGHT PAGE

ISBN CODE: 978-0-578-20638-7

Table of Contents

PREFACE

Through discussions, lectures, laboratory, and theoretical approaches, the subject of Kinesiology can be used in various ways. By designing and implementing physical activity programs, fitness professionals can continue to assist students, athletes, clients, patients, and others to achieve their goals. The Center for Disease Control and Prevention states, 51% of individuals in the United States age 18 years and older meet the physical activity guidelines for aerobic activity. But only 21% percent of adults age 18 and older meet the physical activity guidelines for both aerobic and muscle-strengthening activity. Approximately 60-million people in the United States exercise, but they can't stay with a fitness /exercise program for a long period of time. Some of the reasons for quitting are: a hectic life, no consequences for stopping, starting too fast, too much information, and workouts that are not enjoyable. However, there is hope for all. In this workbook there are some approaches that will assist individuals with various fitness programs for life. The focus is a simple positive-reinforcement intervention called behavioral contracting, which is a self-made contract. The individual plan is easily carried out by the participant; it involves goal setting, pre-planning, creating expectations within yourself, excitement, and a reward system. These pre-planned behavior contracts make it easier to start a fitness/exercise program. The contract has detailed specific goals and it creates achievable goals that bind us mentally. Here are some examples of contract goals:

- "Random Selection" – choosing different exercises for the day by "the luck of a draw", (measurements and assessments page 41 and workbook assignments page 49);
- Keeping objective records, positive reinforcement, and feedback (see charts F.I.T.T. principle charts and various charts in the appendix);
- "Exercise Comfort" – exercise at the same place and the same time;
- "Walk Before You Run" – start an exercise program comfortably with gradual improvements that are best for your fitness level;
- "Exercise with a Partner" (see page 69)

The goal of this workbook is to create a psychological awareness in the area of Kinesiology and Nutrition. This awareness will assist individuals to live a balanced life each day. Once our mind establishes a focus towards achievable fitness goals, we can plan healthier eating habits in conjunction with sustainable workout routines. This does not imply quick nutritional fixes or instant behavioral turnarounds by using bad diet plans, instead it establishes various levels of fitness through "measurements and assessments" and learning how to incorporate nutrition into a fitness plan. Kinesiology is defined as the scientific study of human or non-human body movements. In the arena of physical fitness, Kinesiology is adapted through exercise to improve exercise routines for all individuals. At the conclusion of this workbook, an individual will be able to apply simple concepts of nutrition to their fitness goals, understand the 5 components of physical fitness, and apply fitness concepts using the F.I.T.T. principle. It is important to understand that there are differences in everyone's height, weight, and overall body chemistry; therefore we should not compare ourselves to others. We want to select a fitness routine that is suitable for each specific individual.

PHYSICAL FITNESS

What is physical fitness? Wikipedia informs us that physical fitness is "a measure of the body's ability to perform physical activities without compromising the body and creating health problems." The

Cleveland Clinic notes that exercise can help decrease symptoms of chronic obstructive pulmonary disease, which is a lung ailment that makes breathing difficult. In addition, exercising aids in decreasing blood pressure, blood cholesterol levels, the risk of diabetes, stroke, heart disease, improves mood, anxiety, decreases stress levels, increases muscle endurance, muscle strength, flexibility, and balance. Neurotransmitters and chemicals, such as endorphins, are often called the "feel good chemicals." They are released during extended physical activity and contribute to feelings of calmness and happiness. A healthy way to release tension and negative energy is through exercise.

For individuals who exercise for non-competitive reasons, aerobic exercise allows them to exercise longer. Aerobic exercise is less stressful to the body, creates an exercise comfort zone, results in weight loss, and can be performed over longer periods of time without injury.

If we are looking for more rapid results or improving various fitness goals, anaerobic exercise training is the best choice. Anaerobic exercise refers to the absence of oxygen; during more up-tempo anaerobic exercises, muscles and cells rely on various reactions that do not require oxygen to fuel muscle contraction. Hence, cells produce waste molecules that can impair muscle contractions which can cause a decline in one's performance. This phenomenon is called "the monkey on your back" or fatigue and it is unavoidable when performing anaerobic exercise routines. It also causes added discomfort along with weakened muscles during exercise or competition. It is important to note that when the body is rested the repair process causes muscles to become stronger and more toned.

The Aging Process

Older bodies mean more stiff and tight muscles and joints, which is caused by a combination of physical degeneration and/or inactivity. Although we cannot help getting older, we should continue to improve our flexibility and create or maintain an exercise routine. The aging process should not be an excuse to do nothing. Even though older individuals should be more aware of specific safety measures, the need to exercise more days during the week will create a healthier you. Aging adults should choose exercise routines that are comfortable and safe for their bodies. It is equally important to be patient with your fitness goals so that the body can make proper adjustments mentally and physically.

Researchers with Duke University's School of Medicine suggest that as we age into our 50's, strength, balance, and endurance begin to decline. This is especially true for individuals who do not exercise. This research also reinforces longevity of life by maintaining physical ability. Assistant professor of medicine at Duke and lead author, Katherine Hall, states, "don't wait until you are 80 years old and cannot get out of a chair" she also adds, "our ability to function independently can often be preserved with regular exercise."

A Study at Duke University & the Aging Process

A. More physical activity was associated with less physical decline, especially in ages 60 through 79.
B. Declines in walking speed and aerobic endurance became evident in the 60's and 70's.
C. Both men and women in their 50's began to slip in their ability to stand on one leg and rise from a chair, and the declines continued in the next decade.

MENTAL BENEFITS & THE AGEING PROCESS

We do not realize the overall benefits of exercise as we age and studies continue to show how exercise for the aging plays a vital role. Another exercise health benefit for seniors is the improvement of their mental health as they age. Today, many of us have experienced loved ones who have developed dementia or experienced depression. Did you know that mental health in aging loved ones can take a dangerous turn when we least expect it? Seniors or anyone who is aging can take advantage of the following benefits by just starting up a good exercise routine.

1. Better Sleep - exercise will help the body to relax and enhance your sleep.
2. Improve Thinking Processes – exercise increases the flow of oxygen creating a clearer mind, better memory, and a sharper focus.
3. Improves Mood and Relieve Stress - exercise releases endorphin (chemicals released into your body triggering a positive feeling) which helps with mood, stress, and tension.

Let's Get Started

Let's start our routine by using one or more charts that are located in the F.I.T.T. principle exercise charts (see pages 36-39), the weekly cardiovascular fitness chart (appendix), the food log-in (page 67), static and dynamic stretches for flexibility (pages 10, 132-139), and rubric charts for assessing your progress every 2-3 months (page 129-131). These charts will assist with a quick and safe calorie burning fitness routine. By keeping the heart rate in a calorie burning zone (see page 40), we can cut weight quickly and efficiently. Even though a 3-4 day per week exercise routine along with a good meal plan is a great start, using a 5-6 day per week exercise routine will provide efficient quality results. Lastly, review, read, and incorporate the simple 5 components of physical fitness into your routines (page 8).

Competitive Sports & Advanced Fitness

Over the last 25 years, studies in sports science have changed drastically. Competitive sports and advanced fitness programs use specific workouts and various training methods that are specifically related to their sport. These workouts incorporate elements of agility, power, strength, speed, conditioning, and the importance of nutrition. Programs that include these types of routines create confidence, build stronger bodies, and prepare individuals for competition or personal advanced fitness goals. A good fitness training program should always be well supervised by someone who is experienced. If not, participants could be injured and miss several weeks of training. During this phase training programs should always have upper and lower body strength routines, plyometrics, abilities, and speed training. It is imperative that a proper rest period is included in your exercise routine. This will allow for appropriate recovery of the immune system, muscle repair, and muscle growth. If we don't have a rest and recovery period, exercise routines at a 100% effort cannot happen (page 15).

Even though each competitive sports and advanced fitness program may require specific exercises, the primary focus should be on these categories. Sport competition programs should divide the training into three phases per year:

- Phase 1: Post-Season Training Programs are defined as physical fitness programs that start 2-4 weeks after the season of competition, and last for approximately 1-2 months. Training should always start slowly and gradually.

- Phase 2: Pre-Season Programs are defined as the most crucial area in a physical fitness program. During this phase of 3-8 months, physical fitness programs are in full training mode. This phase includes weight lifting programs that have areas of muscle strength and endurance peaks. This peak area is the phase that most individuals are making their best gains.

- Phase 3: In-Season Programs are defined as physical fitness programs that are used during the actual season of competition. The focus in this phase is maintaining the body's health, strength, and flexibility as much as possible. During this phase, physical fitness routines are usually cut down by 50% - 66%. Workouts may be 20-30 minutes with 2-3 sets of high repetitions (10-15 reps). Since the body is in competition season, most exercise routines in this phase should concentrate on exercises that have limited stress on the body. This will allow muscles, bones, and joints to recuperate for the next competition.

EXERCISE and FITNESS

The 5 Components of Physical Fitness

The 5 primary components of physical fitness are flexibility, cardiovascular exercise, muscular endurance, muscular strength, and body composition. The 5 components of physical fitness combine the necessary ingredients to be in the best physical condition possible. When starting an exercise program, each individual should include these 5 components to achieve the maximum results within their exercise program. The list below gives a brief description of each component that should be used in a physical fitness program.

1. Flexibility

Flexibility is the injury free degree to which a muscle will lengthen. It involves the ability to move a part of the body through a full range of motion which is allowed by a normal disease-free joint. Flexibility or stretching is best represented by how far an individual can reach, bend, and turn. A lack of flexibility can lead to tight muscle, injuries, and joint pain. This is due in part to a limited range of movement. When our muscles are not stretched, the risk of injury becomes greater. We can develop muscular discomfort, muscle tears, and loss of performance. Besides the inability to increase performance, tight muscles may result in a dramatic loss of strength and power during physical activity. The 3 stretches that can drastically help in the flexibility process in a physical fitness program are static, dynamic, and ballistic stretches (see flexibility assessment page 54).

Breathing, Stretching, and Muscle Soreness Connection

We cannot measure total-body flexibility. A simple toe-touching assessment called the sit and reach can be used to measure core flexibility. Stretching during the warm-up and cool-down helps to maintain overall flexibility. Stretching should not be painful, but it will cause some discomfort since the muscles are being stretched beyond their regular length. Because people differ anatomically, comparing one person's flexibility with another's flexibility is not wise. Individuals with poor flexibility who try to stretch as far as others may create injuries.

Muscle soreness can happen with any physical fitness routine, but good breathing control is beneficial during exercise and a good stretch. As you stretch each muscle, exhale, and inhale for 20-30 seconds. This type of breathing technique will help relax the body and increases blood flow throughout the body. It also helps mechanically remove lactic acid and other by-products. For example, exercise routines can lead to tiny injuries called "micro-damage" in the muscle fibers and connective tissue. If a new routine is started a day or two later, muscles will feel sore. "We call that delayed onset muscle soreness. It peaks within about 48 hours, and then it will gradually get better. The good news is that when you do the same activity again, your muscles will start to get used to it. You will actually have no soreness or less soreness because you have strengthened the muscle or connective tissue," says Ethel Frese, PT, DPT, CCS, associate professor of Physical Therapy at St. Louis University. It is important to know that good blood circulation is vital in helping the muscles receive adequate amounts of oxygen and nutrients. But poor circulation increases muscle fatigue and the ability to recover from strenuous exercise.

MUSCLE DIAGRAM FOR MUSCLE SORENESS

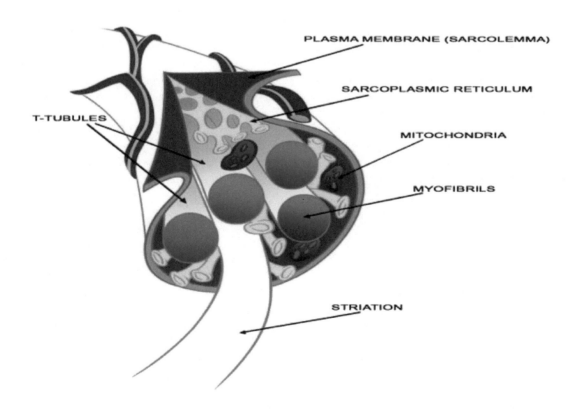

Why Am I Sore?

Performing fitness exercises causes lactic acid accumulation in the muscle, thus causing muscles to become irritated and sore. But after a few hours after a workout, lactic acid is discarded from the muscle. In fact, this muscle soreness is caused by microscopic muscle fiber tears and inflammation. This is called delayed onset muscle soreness (DOMS). DOMS can reduce your strength, create discomfort throughout the body, or difficult to walk for 1-2 days. DOMS can be prevented by gradually and carefully starting a program of your choice. This slow, gradual exercise process allows the muscle time to adjust while the exercises are being done.

How can DOMS be treated?

Even though nothing has been proven to be 100% effective, rest, ice packs, painkillers, and massage may assist in easing DOMS symptoms. If the symptoms are unbearable or too painful, seek a physician's help as soon as possible.

STRETCHING

Most physical fitness, cardiovascular, and weight training programs use basic static, dynamic, and ballistic stretches. Using these types of stretches before and after exercise are the best for creating a better range of motion, various movements in sports, and overall activities for daily living. Better flexibility lessens the possibility of injury. Also, using specific stretches for your type of competition/sport can diminish the likelihood of injury. One example is to create a competitive situation with the muscle used. The more the muscle is stretched and utilized for the competitive situation, the more the muscles become accustomed to that particular movement. For example: Falling down and exploding upwards use dynamic and ballistic type stretching movements. Stretching these muscle areas can be of tremendous benefit due to these types of stretching movements.

Static Stretches

Static stretching is the most common type of stretch. Overall the static stretch is safe and is one of the best stretches for improving flexibility. It is usually held for a 20-30 second count. A static stretch is maintained until an individual feels a comfortable, but solid snug within the muscle being stretched.

Dynamic Stretches

Today dynamic stretching is being used more than ever before. In competitive sports and physical fitness this stretch is performed as an individual simultaneously moves and stretches, but the stretch is not held for a specific amount of time. Dynamic stretching is most effective when the stretch relates to a particular movement for the specific sport.

Ballistic Stretches

If not used with good solid warm up and a proper stretch routine, ballistic stretches can be dangerous. They are stretches which use small bouncing movements to force the stretched muscle passed its normal range of motion. But by putting this extra bouncing pressure on the muscle and tendons, the muscles could pull, strain, or tear causing possible injury. Individuals using ballistic stretches should always stretch with a certified coach or trainer.

2. Cardiovascular Exercise

Cardiovascular exercise is essential to a physical fitness routine. A simple cardiovascular training routine can create a healthier you within weeks. As obesity levels climb worldwide, it's becoming apparent that fewer individuals fully appreciate the benefits of an efficient cardiovascular system. The following are 31 benefits as outlined by Dr. Michael Olpin of Weber State University:

1) Increase in blood vessel diameter.
   - Blood flows more easily.
   - Blood pressure decreases during rest.
   - Decreased risk of potentially life-threatening blood clots.
2) Increased Cardiac Output.
   - More blood per beat ejected from the heart.
   - Greater levels of oxygen and nutrients into the cells.
   - Greater blood flow to the muscles (recorded as up to 88% of blood flows to the muscles during high-intensity aerobic activity.
   - Increase the strength of heart contraction resulting in a less-stressed heart muscle.
3) Decreased Resting Heart Rate.
   - Less stress on the heart.
   - Decreased heart rate (potentially 10 bpm translating into 5,256,000 fewer beats/year.
4) Decreased Maximum Heart Rate Output.
   - The heart (muscle) doesn't have to work as hard to do the same amount of work as an unconditioned heart.
5) Increased Heart Chambers, resulting from a stronger heart.
6) Increase in stroke volume (volume of blood ejected per beat) resulting in a lower pulse and stronger heart contraction, and less stress on the heart.
7) Lower chance of dysrhythmias (abnormal heartbeat) of the electrical conduction in the heart, making it more likely the heart will beat normally.
8) Lower blood pressure in both resting systolic, diastolic, and mean blood pressure as well as during maximum load.
9) Decrease in peripheral resistance.
10) Increase in the number of red blood cells, thus providing more oxygen-carrying capacity from the lungs to the cells.
11) Increase in capillarization as noted by a decrease in the surface area within capillaries.

- An increase in the transport of oxygen and other nutrients into the cells from the blood vessels. This translates into more areas for nutrients to find the cells.

12) Long-term flexibility in blood vessels, resulting in multiple benefits.

13) Enhanced clotting and anti-clotting mechanisms.
- faster blood clotting post-exercise as well as faster un-clotting.
- reduced risk of arteriosclerosis.
- A substance called plasminogen is converted into plasmin to help dissolve clots. To activate the plasminogen so that it becomes plasmin, the cells that line the blood vessels produce a substance called tissue plasminogen activator - tPA (tPA - is a protein involved in the breakdown of blood clots). Fit people produce more tPA than unfit people.

14) Thanks to increased blood hemoglobin levels both Oxygen and carbon dioxide (waste matter) are efficiently transported through the system.

15) Blood plasma volume is significantly improved.

16) Cardiac tissue becomes stronger – meaning greater heart efficiency in the short- and long-term.

17) Increased anaerobic threshold allows for exercise both longer and at a higher level before lactic acid can build up.

18) Increased efficiency of blood coagulation (hemoconcentration) results in faster clotting of blood following injury.

19) Increased blood volume (up to 25%) results in more oxygen and nutrients transported to cells.

20) Decrease of plaque buildup along the walls of arteries.

21) Reduced risk of hypertension (high blood pressure).

22) Reduced rate and severity of medical complications associated with hypertension.

23) Offsets some negative side-effects of many antihypertensive drugs.

24) Increased blood transport to the brain.
- Higher brain capillary volume.
- During one study, exercising subjects were "more aroused, alert, and engaged" compared with non-exercisers.

25) Increased respiratory muscle strength and endurance, especially important for asthmatics.

26) Increase in capillary density near skeletal and cardiac muscle characterized by:
- an increase in myoglobin stores.
- an increase in the number of capillaries surrounding muscle tissue.
- an increase in mitochondrial "reticulum."
- an increase in the size and number of mitochondria (powerhouse of the cell).
- allows more oxygen to be absorbed into the muscle cells.
- transports more nutrients to the tissues.
- permits greater levels of aerobic work.

27) Decreases levels of the protein known as C-reactive protein (CRP) in the body. Evidence shows that people with high levels of this protein appear to have a higher than average risk of cardiovascular disease. A recent study suggested that testing for CRP could be an even better

predictor of heart attack than high cholesterol. SOURCE: Arteriosclerosis, Thrombosis, and Vascular Biology 2002; 22:1869-1876.

28) Thinning of the blood allowing the heart not to work as hard.
29) Improved potential of surviving a heart attack.
30) Decreased risk of stroke.
31) Decreases overall risk of heart disease probably more than any other single factor.

3. Muscular Endurance

Muscular Endurance is the ability of a muscle or muscle group to either contract many times and/or maintain a position for an extended amount of time. Increased metabolism, better posture, limited tiredness, and a reduced chance of injury represent some of the benefits. Muscle endurance exercises can help you maintain a healthy weight, or with a proper diet plan, it can help lose weight. Physical exercise burns calories as you expend energy with each movement. Your metabolic rate also increases with physical activity and remains elevated even while at rest. This burns more calories for weight loss even when you are not active. The National Strength and Conditioning Association recommends performing resistance exercises such as plyometrics, weightlifting, or using your body weight, at 12 or more repetitions per exercise. It is suggested to use 2 to 3 sets of each exercise, and rest 15-20 seconds or less between sets. For the best result in muscle endurance training use 12 stations at 67 percent (.67 x 100 lbs. = your one rep bench press maximum). During everyday activities, muscle endurance exercise gives you more energy. Walking up the stairs, lifting various objects, running errands, and other daily tasks become much more comfortable. Muscular endurance exercises can help increase muscle strength and tone. Muscular endurance exercises involving high repetitions while adding small increments of weight can improve muscular strength. However, for the best strength training and muscle mass, heavier weight and low repetition programs are the best and can create maximum muscle gains.

Bones and Joints

Muscular endurance goes further than just improving the health of your muscles. One of the most ignored areas of the body when weight training is our bones and joints. All ages can benefit from physical fitness programs that include muscular endurance training. Reports by Dr. Vivian H. Heyward, author of "Advanced Fitness Assessment and Exercise Prescription" say there are beneficial effects to muscle endurance training, and it may decrease the risk of osteoporosis and bone fractures.

Muscle Endurance and Competitive Sports

When using training programs that involve muscular endurance training competitive sports individuals can last longer in competition before fatigue settles in. When performing muscle endurance exercises during an in-season exercise program, the fatigue level is limited. Muscle endurance training allows the muscles to support loads of efficient energy for more extended periods. Any individual or team who has the chance of boosting their endurance should take advantage of the opportunity.

4. Muscular Strength

Strengthening your muscles takes dedication, hard work, and consistency. Muscular strength is the amount of force a muscle or muscle group can exert. With stronger muscles, higher muscle mass and optimal muscular strength, we seem to function for more extended periods of time without becoming fatigued. Muscular strength decreases fatty tissues, increases skeletal muscle, improves basal metabolic rate, and enhances the metabolism of dietary nutrients. People who have large amounts of muscle mass tend to have high athletic endurance and physical stability. These individuals tend to have better sleep cycles and improved mental concentration. Several studies indicate that muscular strength and regular physical activity is required to maintain overall health and well-being. Many studies also suggested that a variety of medical diseases such as cancer, cardiovascular disease, diabetes, high cholesterol, hypertension, and hormonal disorders can be prevented with physical activity and "resistance training" exercises. When our muscles become stronger, we adapt more to the physical and environmental stressors. This strength helps by decreasing the risk of injury in repetitive or sudden movements. This is especially advantageous for athletes who are at a higher risk of developing trauma due to excessive stressful muscular and joint motion.

A Healthier Older Me

As we advance in age strong muscles, contribute to healthy bones and joints by promoting healthy remodeling of bones. Individuals who continue to work out will maintain muscular strength and tend to age slowly. Their risk of developing fractures, osteoporosis, or other defects of bone mineral density decrease. If we have certain medical conditions, promoting muscle mass may decrease the progression of illness. Enhancing muscular strength with exercise can help reduce diabetes significantly. Research and clinical data show that diabetics who strength train respond better to insulin, improve blood sugar levels, lose weight, and lower the risk for heart disease. When partnered with cardiovascular exercises, muscular strength and resistance exercises decrease the possibility of cardiovascular diseases. People who have an excellent muscular strength program are less likely to develop hypertension, a high concentration of fats or lipids in the blood, promote better breathing functions, and prevent the development of constipation.

Enhanced Posture

Since most posture issues are caused by muscular imbalances, poor posture can manifest into many different conditions. As the larger groups of muscles develop in strength training, the smaller group of muscles and connective tissue become stronger and more capable of handling stress and strain within the body. With overall muscular strength in large and small muscle groups, we can enhance our posture and alignment of connective tissues. Thus, performing the correct weight exercises can significantly improve posture.

5. Body Composition

Body composition is defined as the comparison of fat in the body and lean muscle mass. For the best results in body composition testing, we must have a solid exercise routine 4-5 days a week. We can measure body composition by using a device called a skin fold caliper. A skinfold caliper is the least expensive and the most widely available methods for body composition testing. It involves pinching specific areas of skin and fat throughout the body and converting the results into an estimate of body fat percentage (see page 50-53). Calipers do provide us with body fat assessments, but they do not measure deep belly fat which is very important regarding health. Also, the test is very dependent on an experienced person and the quality of the calipers used. For the best results caliper measurements and assessments along with a solid exercise program should be performed every 4-8 weeks.

MENTAL and PHYSICAL BARRIERS in PHYSICAL FITNESS

There always seems to be some kind of brick wall that blocks a fitness program. Just as our minds and bodies become adjusted to a fitness workout schedule, something or someone puts a wrench in the program. To conquer these barriers, we must find alternatives that will aid us in staying focused on our fitness routine. One of the hardest things to do in physical fitness is to start and stop repeatedly. The famous martial arts teacher and movie star Bruce Lee once said, "missing 1 week of an exercise routine is the same as missing an entire month." If you have ever started an intense fitness program and have stopped for a week or more, I'm sure you remember the soreness, stiffness, and how psychologically tough it was to start back up. Here are some barriers that have caused many individuals to stop their fitness routine.

Not Listening to Your Body

"Be Careful and Listen to your Body" is a term used in physical fitness (see the overtraining syndrome chart below). It is a result of excessive training that creates extreme muscle soreness along with inadequate rest and recovery. This process of extreme muscle soreness can occur quickly after several days of continuous hard training. This area of the overtraining threshold chart has positive and negative effects. Whether it is beginning, intermediate, or advanced training, the area of "progressive" workouts over several days allows the body to be prepared for performance while developing a tolerance for competition or the next workout. Highly intense workouts are an important component for training individuals to peak at competition time; this type of training with proper rest, recovery, and nutrient intake can create a high fitness level. Short-term progressive intense workouts, along with proper rest periods, can bring about significant power and strength gains. It is important to note that following intense workouts, muscle soreness, and fatigue are normal outcomes following a series of intense workouts. If soreness and fatigue are never completely resolved, performance will consistently decline and may be an indicator of "overtraining syndrome."

OVERTRAINING SYNDROME CHART

SYMPTOMS THAT I MAY BE OVERTRAINING		
Psychological Symptoms	**Physiological Symptoms**	**Performance Issues**
• Emotional • Loss of competitive drive • Irritation or anger • Feelings of depression • Concentration difficulties	• Loss of appetite • Constant fatigue • Increase in injuries due to overuse • Constant muscle soreness • Too much weight loss • Irregular menstrual cycles • Increased resting heart rate • Sleep difficulties • Frequent infections or colds	• Delayed recovery • Fatigue earlier than normal • Increased heart rate with limited effort • Decreased speed, endurance, and strength • Decreased aerobic capacity • Altered coordination

If we don't listen to our body and over train, it will lead to physical and psychological tear down. Forcing hard workouts without proper rest not only decreases the chance of improved performance, but it increases the risk of injury. Body improvement is directly tied to the philosophy of rest, recovery, and ingesting the proper nutrients and liquids. Some competitive adolescent male and female athletes do not increase their strength and endurance because coaches and trainers do not allow enough periods of rest and recovery following intense training sessions. One of the top exercise nutrition experts in the world, Dr. John Berardi, states that after a hard work out a given muscle will not fully recover for 7 to 14 days. However, we can resume a workout after 48 hours of rest. If sufficient rest is not given, then we cannot expect a 100% maximum effort during an intense workout or practice.

Overtraining may occur anytime during different training routines and this can result in extreme fatigue, illness, stress fractures, heat exhaustion, and various disabilities.

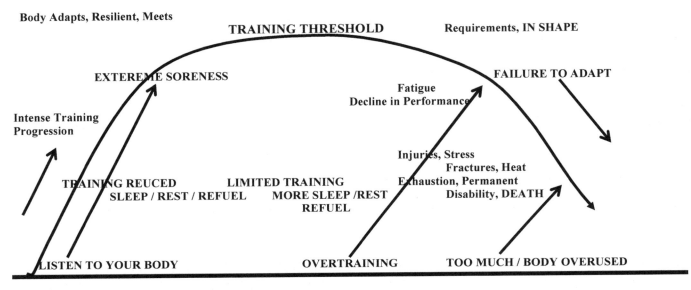

TRAINING THRESHOLD CURVE

INJURIES

The Silent Killer

Abuse, damage, fracture, loss, agony, hemorrhage, ill, misery, mutilation, stab, and suffering are synonyms to the word "injury." Do we really want injuries? When we are injured these words play a significant role in our psychological mood. Sadly enough, injuries will put an end to your excitement and stop you from reaching your goals. Let it be known that we must always give 100% effort in our workout routines. With proper supervision, 100% effort creates stronger muscles, increased body tone, weight loss or weight gain, and various types of progressive improvements; however, to accomplish these individual goals, we must stay as injury free as possible. Even though injuries can come from anywhere, we should be proactive in avoiding additional injuries due to "overtraining."

Balanced Fitness Routines

The 5 physical fitness components as described in this book must be the focal point of your program. For maximum results, do not focus entirely on one component but ensure you are practicing all 5 in a balanced manner. By practicing balance of the 5 components, your body will adjust rapidly to varying workouts, rather than the same old workouts over and over again. During your exercise sessions, continuously remind yourself to give 100% effort and demand your body to thrive toward maximum efforts.

Regularity

It is important to rest, sleep, diet properly, and workout 4-5 times a week. Keep in mind that both specificity and variety are critical; you should have specific goals in all areas of your workout, modify those goals annually, and provide variety in your workouts to meet your goals. This decreases the possibility of stagnating peaks in the flow of your fitness program and it also maintains a positive state of mind. It is suggested that every 2-3 months your fitness program should be modified with various changes. A revised program can prevent injuries, create rejuvenation, decrease plateaus in weight gain or loss, prevent stagnate muscles, conquer workout boredom, and keep your brain focused.

Proper Equipment

If you feel comfortable during exercise, there is a greater chance you are more encouraged to exercise. Proper clothing is a key factor and supports your body in different areas. Feeling good in your clothes boosts confidence, creates a positive feeling about exercise, and aids in the willpower to stay focused on your fitness routine each day. When choosing clothing, make sure it enables you to move freely during compound exercises and stretching routines, fits comfortably, and feels good. Some individuals may not understand the importance of a good shoe; however, proper exercise shoes can improve your performance, assist in balance, and can support you to make quick directional changes. For the best balance and support here are some important points to consider when choosing your training shoes.

- Get the proper size; wrong size = slipping and blisters which slows you down.
- Comfortable support and cushion.
- Orthotic inserts may be needed to correct balance and support.
- Improper selection of shoes could lead to injuries such as: sprains, fractures, bunions, corns, etc.

FITNESS FOR LIFE

Nutrition

Knowing what to eat, how much to eat, and how to choose an array of foods with nutritional value can be confusing. When we are hungry, our brains initiate a physiological response that prompts us to seek food for the energy and nutrients that our bodies require to maintain proper functioning. Appetite is a learned psychological desire to consume food. Many factors influence our mental drive to eat, including: cultural and social meanings attached to food, convenience, advertising, habit, customs, emotions, perceived nutritional value, social interactions, and financial means. Our nutrition and what we consume is responsible for strong healthy muscles. We must always be aware that the consumption of a significant amount of carbohydrates does not promote muscle mass, but instead it gives us the energy to create the muscle mass. Competitive and non-competitive athletes should consume more calories from proteins than carbohydrates. In this workbook, you will learn how to calculate the percentages of proteins, carbohydrates, and fats in your diet. As an athlete or someone looking to stay fit, we must understand that the body's consumption of calories must be higher than the amount burned. If we are consuming fewer calories than we burn during the day, we interfere with creating strength, power, and muscle mass.

The nutrients we must stay focused on while exercising are proteins, carbohydrates, and fats. Other nutrients such as vitamins and trace minerals are needed in smaller amounts, these are called micronutrients. Before the body can use foods, the digestive system must break down the more substantial food particles into smaller more usable forms.

Vitamins and Minerals

The best source of daily vitamins is through the foods we eat; however, studies show that one multivitamin taken daily can ensure our body receives the essential nutrients required to function properly. Deficiencies in any of these vitamins can possibly cause problems within your body. Let's consider your body to be an automobile; gasoline, oil, transmission fluid, brake fluid, and spark plugs are essential for the car to operate. If your car receives these items, it will function properly and last longer, your body is much the same. Vitamins are molecules that are needed throughout your body to create a specific reaction. They are the essential organic compounds that promote growth and help to maintain life and health. Every essential vitamin you need can be found in the foods you eat or by taking vitamin supplements. The problem is many of us don't eat enough of these foods or none at all which causes the body to react to insufficiencies.

Society has become so fast-paced that many people are replacing healthy meals with fast foods. We don't realize how our fast food choices lack the essential vitamins our body needs to function properly. As our bodies become older, we begin to lose specific physiological functions. Maintaining good eating habits and taking our essential vitamins can help delay potential loss in body functions. Bone loss, memory, and eyesight are some physiological functions that can be lost during the ageing process. However, all these functions can be maintained and made stronger by taking in the necessary vitamins our body needs.

The 10 Most Important Vitamins

1. Vitamin A: A fat-soluble vitamin that is an important factor in maintaining a healthy immune system. Best food source for vitamin A is liver; however, it is recommended that you only consume liver once or twice a month. Other food sources are cheese, egg yolk, skim milk, and butter. Recommended daily allowance is 4,000-5,000 IU (International Units)

2. Vitamin B-1: This vitamin is also known as thiamin. It is excellent for the nervous system and energy metabolism. Thiamin can be found in peas, pork, whole grains, and liver. YUM! The deficiency of this vitamin can lead to mental diseases, muscle weakness, and wasting of both mind and body.

3. B-2 Vitamins: Commonly known as riboflavin help energy metabolism, healthy skin, and good vision. You can find Riboflavin in milk, liver, whole grain products, eggs, and green vegetables. A lack of this vitamin can lead to light sensitivity, dermatitis, and unsightly cracks at the corners of your mouth.

4. Vitamin B-6: This water-soluble vitamin is part of the vitamin B complex group. Several forms of the vitamin are known, but pyridoxal phosphate (PLP) is the active form and is a cofactor in many reactions of amino acid in the metabolism. B-6 can be found in Brussel sprouts, bananas, cabbage, fish, (most) leafy green vegetables, liver, mayonnaise, meat, soybean, canola and olive oils, nuts and seeds, potatoes and sweet potatoes, minerals, poultry, whole-grain and fortified cereals, iodine, and iodized salt.

5. Vitamin B-12: This vitamin plays a vital role in the normal functioning of the brain and nervous system, and for the formation of blood. It is generally involved in the metabolism of every cell of the human body, especially affecting DNA synthesis and regulation, but also fatty acid synthesis and energy production. It is the largest and most structurally complicated vitamin. Vitamin B-12 can be found in saltwater fish, shellfish, eggs, magnesium, fortified cereals, cocoa and chocolate, dark meat, green vegetables, (most) milk and milk products, dry beans, peas, lentils, organ meats, fish, nuts, and seeds.

6. Vitamin C: This is important to help boost our immune system. The best foods to get vitamin C are citrus fruit, strawberries, cantaloupe, kiwi, potatoes, and sweet peppers.

7. Vitamin D: Important in absorbing calcium which is essential to prevent bone loss or bone weakness. Getting sufficient sunlight is the best source of vitamin D, but other sources are found in milk fortified with vitamin D, eggs, peanuts, peanut butter, egg yolk, whole grains, fortified cereals, fortified milk, phosphorus, liver, dry beans, peas, lentils high-fatty fish, and eggs.

8. Folic Acid: This is a B vitamin found in kidneys, livers, meats, whole grains, fish, and green vegetables. This vitamin helps build your protein metabolism and healthy red blood cells. It is an essential factor in preventing heart disease and birth defects.

9. Vitamin K: This helps blood clot as well as help to build and strengthen bone. The best source of Vitamin K is in green leafy vegetables such as spinach, broccoli, cabbage, and turnip greens. The recommended daily allowance for Vitamin K is 45-60 mcg for an adult.

10. Niacin: A "B" vitamin essential for producing energy, creating a healthy appetite, and sustaining healthy nerves and skin. To get more Niacin in your diet plan, try eating more fish, poultry, liver meat, and peanuts. A lack of this vitamin can lead to skin rashes and weakness of the body and mind.

The 12 Important Minerals

Minerals are inorganic (non-living), indestructible elements that aid in the physiological processes within the body. Without minerals, vitamins could not be absorbed. Like vitamins, minerals are substances found in food that your body needs for growth and health. There are two kinds of minerals called macro-minerals and trace minerals.

6 Macro-minerals

1. Calcium: Our body needs calcium for forming bones and teeth. Calcium also helps nerves and muscles function. An over consumption of carbonated soft drinks can cause your body to excrete extra calcium, which can cause calcium loss from your bones. Foods that contain calcium are Chinese cabbage, bok choy, kale, collard, and canned salmon with bones, sardines, milk, cheese, yogurt, greens, turnip greens, mustard greens, broccoli, and calcium-fortified orange juice.

2. Chloride: The body needs chloride for keeping the water balanced in the different parts of your body. Foods that contain chloride are beef, pork, rye, tomatoes, lettuce, celery, olives, cheese, salt, seaweed, and sardines.

3. Magnesium: The body needs magnesium for healthy nerve and muscle function and forming bones and teeth. Foods that contain magnesium are seafood, yogurt, bran cereal, green leafy vegetables, nuts, cheese, and milk.

4. Phosphorus: The body needs phosphorus for storing energy from foods and forming bones and teeth. Foods that contain phosphorous are bread, some cereals, milk, red meat, yogurt, cheese, poultry, fish, eggs, nuts, and peas.

5. Potassium: The body needs potassium for healthy nerve and muscle function and to keep the right amounts of water in the various parts of your body. Foods that contain potassium are melons, potatoes, sweet potatoes, prunes, milk, bananas, tomatoes, oranges, raisins, spinach, turnip greens, salt substitutes (potassium chloride), most peas and beans, collard greens, and kale.

6. Sodium: The body needs sodium for keeping equal amounts of water in the different parts of your body and healthy nerve and muscle function. Sodium is necessary for various metabolic functions, the transmission of nerve impulses, regulation of blood and body fluids, and heart activity. Most of American diets have sodium but come from highly processed foods which enhance with sodium as a preservative and to add flavor. Some studies show a link between sodium intake and hypertension (high blood pressure). They have now set the milligrams of sodium intake to 2,300 milligrams per day. Foods that contain sodium are green olives, beets, salt, milk, cheese, celery, sardines, beef, and pork

6 Trace Minerals

1. Copper: The body needs copper to help protect cells from damage, and to form bone and red blood cells. Foods that contain copper are chocolate, mushrooms, nuts, beans, shellfish (especially oysters), whole-grain cereals, and organ meats.

2. Fluoride: The body needs fluoride for forming bones and teeth. Foods that contain fluoride are tea, coffee, fluoridated water and, saltwater fish.

3. Iodine: The body needs iodine for thyroid gland function. Foods that contain iodine are iodized, drinking water and salt seafood.

4. Iron: The body needs iron to help muscles function and for red blood cells to deliver oxygen to body tissues. Iron deficiency is the most common deficiency in the world. Iron deficiency frequently leads to anemia which results from the body's inability to produce hemoglobin. Foods that contain iron are fish, liver, soybean flour, eggs, beans, molasses, spinach, fortified breakfast cereals, turnip greens, lentils, red meats, poultry, peas, clams, whole grains, and dried fruit (apricots, prunes, and raisins).

5. Selenium: The body needs selenium for thyroid function and to help protect cells from damage. Foods that contain selenium are grains, eggs, brewer's yeast, wheat germ, chicken, liver, garlic, vegetables, fish, shellfish, red meat, and enriched bread.

6. Zinc: The body needs zinc to assist in fighting off illnesses and infections, for healthy skin, and to heal wounds. Foods that contain zinc are whole grains, fortified cereals, wheat, liver, eggs, seafood, red meats, oysters, beans, peas, lentils, peanuts, nuts, certain seafood, and milk products.

THE IMPORTANCE OF WATER CONSUMPTION

Water is a crucial nutrient. Humans can survive much longer without food than without water. Dehydration, the abnormal depletion of body fluids, can cause severe problems in a matter of hours. The human body consists of 50 to 70 percent water by weight. An individual's need for water varies drastically according to: dietary factors, age, size, overall health, environmental temperature, humidity levels, and exercise. Most people can meet their hydration needs by merely eating a healthy diet and drinking when thirsty. General consumption recommendations are for men, 13 cups, and women, 9 cups, of total water each day, both of which can be consumed from water, other beverages, and food.

The proper consumption of water throughout the day helps to cleanse your body. Never go a day without drinking a minimum of eight 8-oz of water per day for a total of 64-oz. The benefits can include:

- Weight loss
- Cleansing (*water flushes down the by-products of fat breakdown*)
- Hunger reduction (*water is a very effective appetite suppressant; thus, you eat less*)
- Zero calorie intake
- Better looks (*water hydrates the skin, making your skin healthier and younger looking as it helps to replenish skin tissues, moisturizes the skin, and increase skin elasticity*)
- More energy (*water relieves fatigue*)
- Cancer vulnerability (*water reduces the risk of cancer that is related to the digestive system. Some studies show that drinking a healthy amount of water may reduce the risks of bladder and colon cancer. Additionally, water dilutes the concentration of cancer-causing agents in the urine and shortens the time in which they are in contact with the lining of the bladder.*)
- Improved physical performance (*During physical activity, water can lower your maximum heart rate, improve endurance, reduce fatigue, and helps soreness after exercise.*)

- Boosts your mood with positive emotions
- Boosts your brainpower *(drinking water improves your thinking performance)*

Weight Gain and Weight Loss

Individuals who start a new program often start too fast expecting a quick fix. This may eventually lead to frustration when results are not seen immediately. As a result, some will quit, lose weight, gain weight, and will tend to use a variety of diet plans hoping for temporary fixes. A realistic approach requires time, and a legitimate plan lasting at least a year. The one-year plan will be fun, provide less pressure, and it will motivate one to learn about nutrition and other various exercise programs.

Becoming more aware of who you are, what you are becoming, and how you got there should create an awakening in your soul. But first, we must be able to apply some basic information about nutritional needs. Using the Mifflin-St. Jeor equation, energy resources from foods, vitamins, minerals, and a solid achievable physical fitness program, we can add or cut calories and be fit for life. Hence, the principle of a fit for life program must focus on discipline, physical fitness, and putting healthy learned behaviors into practice.

- Energy In = Intake of Food
- Energy Out = Burning of Calories (basic exercises)

Energy In > Energy Out = Weight Gain

Gaining Weight

Once you know the number of calories needed to maintain your weight (using the Mifflin-St. Jeor equation page 24) you can calculate the number of calories you need to gain weight. To increase body weight, consume more calories than you burn. For example, if 2,500 calories are required to maintain your weight, then eating an extra 500 calories per day will cause you to gain weight. Nutrition plans can be found throughout the internet. Various calorie counter applications are available to assist you in keeping track of your daily caloric intake as well as tracking total protein, carbohydrates, and fats. Using one of these tools, we can add and replace foods for any plan based on desired goals. Below is an example of a healthy weight gain meal can look like (based on calorie needs some males or females may need more or less).

BEFORE BREAKFAST
1 scoop whey protein (mix in water)
1 medium banana

BREAKFAST
3 whole eggs + 3 egg whites
2 cups cooked oatmeal
2 slices 100 whole wheat toast

POSTWORKOUT SNACK
2 scoops whey protein

1 medium plain bagel + 2 Tbsp. jelly

MORNING SNACK
8 oz. low-fat cottage cheese + 1 cup sliced pineapple
6 whole-wheat crackers + 1 Tbsp. peanut butter

LUNCH
8 oz. turkey deli meat
4 slices whole-wheat bread (make sandwiches; feel free to add low-fat mayo and/or mustard)
2 cups green salad + 2 Tbsp. low-fat balsamic vinaigrette

AFTERNOON SNACK
1 scoop whey protein (mix in water)
1 large apple

DINNER
8 oz. top sirloin
1 large sweet potato
1 cup chopped broccoli
2 cups green salad +2 Tbsp. salad dressing (olive oil and vinegar)

Energy In < Energy Out = Weight Loss

Losing Weight

If you want to lose weight, a useful guideline for lowering your caloric intake is to reduce your calories by at least 250-500, but not more than 1,000 below your maintenance level. The American College of Sports Medicine (ACSM) recommends that calorie levels never drop below 1,200 calories per day for women or 1,800 calories per day for men (even these calorie levels are quite low). An alternative way of calculating a safe caloric-intake level is by using your current body weight and reducing calories by 15-20% below your daily calorie maintenance needs. This percentage may increase depending upon your weight loss goals. Keeping up with your weight loss goals requires self-discipline and attentiveness toward your calorie consumption each day. By using calorie equations (see below) and using various combinations of healthy choices with each meal, one can have good healthy meals every day. More importantly stay below or equal to your calculated calories and exercise 4-5 times per week, and the success of losing weight will come more readily. Use the following healthy food choices below to balance a nutrition plan (for the best choices use "The Most and Least Desired Glycemic Foods" chart on page 32).

Proteins: The foods that are high in protein are: eggs (preferable egg whites or use 1 whole egg remember the yolks are high in cholesterol), fish of your choice, skinless chicken, lean red meat, nuts, soy milk, tofu, pumpkin seeds, sunflower seeds, yogurt, low fat milk, low fat cottage cheese.

Carbohydrates: Whole grains like: barley, bulgur, buckwheat, quinoa, oats, whole wheat, whole grain breads, brown rice, white rice, potatoes, whole wheat pasta or multigrain pasta, fruits, vegetables, beans, lentils, dried peas, whole grain cereals (100% bran), and oatmeal.

Salads: Romaine Lettuce has the best overall nutritional values over other lettuce varieties. Choose dressings that are vinaigrette based rather than cream based.

Drinks: Consume more water than sugary drinks, be sure to get at least eight 8 oz. glasses per day (64oz.). Other options are fruit and vegetable juices with ingredients such as: carrots, cucumber, celery, kale, spinach, romaine lettuce, concord grape juice, fresh lemon juice in water, or make your own smoothie. Moderation is the key when craving sweet drinks, don't overdo it.

Three Great Smoothie Recipes: *(blend all ingredients together until smooth.)*

- Blueberry Banana Smoothie
    - ✓ 1 ¼ cup orange juice
    - ✓ 1 medium ripe banana
    - ✓ 1 cup frozen blueberries, blackberries, or raspberries
    - ✓ 1 cup ice cubes
    - ✓ 8oz lemon yogurt

- Virgin Piña Colada Smoothie
    - ✓ 1 banana
    - ✓ 1 cup diced fresh pineapple
    - ✓ 1 cup pineapple juice
    - ✓ ½ cup "lite" coconut milk
    - ✓ 1 cup ice cubes
    - ✓ 8 oz. Pina Colada yogurt

- Tropical Mango Smoothie
    - ✓ ½ cup pineapple juice
    - ✓ 1 cup diced mango
    - ✓ 1 banana
    - ✓ 2 teaspoon fresh lime juice
    - ✓ ½ tsp. grated, peeled fresh ginger
    - ✓ 1 cup ice cubes
    - ✓ 8oz orange yogurt.

Energy In = Energy Out = Weight stays at a balanced state

Caloric intake equations can be used to determine resting energy expenditure for a human. Resting energy expenditure is the energy necessary to sustain life and to keep our brain, heart, kidneys, liver, lungs, and other organs functioning properly. According to the book Nutrition Therapy and Pathophysiology, the average North American's resting energy expenditure accounts for about 60 to 75-percent of their total daily energy expenditure. The remaining energy expenditure is from 25-percent physical activity and 10-percent of our metabolic process of digesting food. Today, the Mifflin-St. Jeor equation is highly recommended among the nutrition professionals and The American Dietetic Association for estimating caloric needs and predicting resting energy expenditure within 10-percent.

Using the Mifflin-St. Jeor Equation, we can calculate basal metabolic rate (BMR). The basal metabolic rate is the amount of energy expended per day at rest. Once you know your BMR number of calories, you can easily calculate the number of calories needed to gain or lose weight. These equations are very useful, but individuals who are very muscular and those with fast metabolisms may have higher caloric needs. Thus, adding more calories to a diet will create a weight balance or weight gain. Over-weight individuals may have an overestimate of calories and should gradually subtract calories to balance their needs.

STEP 1: Find BMR by using the "Mifflin-St. Jeor" equation

- Females = 10 x (Weight in kg) + 6.25 x (Height in cm) - 5 x age – 161
- Males = 10 x (Weight in kg) + 6.25 x (Height in cm) - 5 x age + 5

STEP 2: Multiply the physical activity levels below for daily caloric needs (estimate only).

- If you are sedentary (little or no exercise) = BMR x 1.2
- If you are lightly active (light exercise/sports 1-3 days/week) = BMR x 1.375
- If you are moderately active (moderate exercise/sports 3-5 days/week) = BMR x 1.55
- If you are very active (hard exercise/sports 6-7 days a week) = BMR x 1.725
- If you are extra active (very hard exercise/sports & physical job or 2x training) = BMR x 1.9

STEP 3: Find Weight Gains vs Weight Loss

- For weight gain = add more caloric consumption to the Mifflin-St. Jeor equation (step 1 & step 2).
- For weight loss = subtract additional caloric consumption from the Mifflin-St. Jeor equation (found in step 1 & 2; start with subtraction of 250 and up).
- Logging in Your Daily Meals for 2-4 Weeks (page 67 for daily food log)

Logging in Meals for 2-4 Weeks

Today, there are several online applications we can use to calculate our daily consumption of foods, but for the best results log your meal plan, calculate your daily consumption of foods, and count the calories for 2-4 weeks. Knowledge of how many calories you are putting into your body can stimulate your mind to stay on track with your goals. If you become bored with the same meal plan and decide to change meals drastically, simply repeat the meal logs for 2-4 weeks again with different foods. This log-in process helps create balanced meals, knowledge of calorie consumption, and awareness of your proteins, carbohydrates, fats, vitamins, and minerals. Lastly, small healthy snacks are more important than you think. Morning and afternoon snacks between breakfast and dinner will help with portion control at lunch and dinner. Find your favorite snacks and use them to prevent sugar cravings and high calorie meals (daily food log page 67).

PROTEINS

Proteins, also referred to as bodybuilders, are a major component of every cell. They help to repair tissue, assist with antibody production and hormone formation. Proteins are broken down by the body into smaller nitrogen-containing molecules known as amino acids. 20-essential amino acids must be obtained from the diet. 11 of the 20-amino acids are considered non-essential because the body can make them on its own. Animal proteins are high-quality proteins which are called complete proteins and supply all the essential amino acids needed. Plant source proteins are called incomplete proteins because they lack one or two of the essential amino acids. By eating complementary plant proteins, we can supply ourselves with all the essential amino acids needed, examples of some complementary plant proteins are:

- salads made with beans, nuts, or seeds
- peanut butter sandwich on whole-grain bread
- hummus with whole-wheat pita bread
- tofu or tempeh with brown rice or quinoa
- tofu stir-fry with whole-grain noodles and peanuts
- beans and brown rice
- yogurt with sunflower seeds or almonds

CALCULATE THE RECOMMENDED DAILY ALLOWANCE OF PROTEINS PER DAY

EQUATION FOR GRAMS OF PROTEINS PER DAY

Example

- STEP #1 = weight = 205lbs
- STEP #2: 205 lbs. ÷ 2.2 = 93kg
- STEP #3 = 93Kg x 1.3 (activity level 6 days per week none-vegetarian endurance workout) = 120.9 grams of protein per day

EQUATION #1: FIND USA RECOMMENDAED PROTEIN GRAMS / BODY WEIGHT

- STEP #1: WHAT IS YOUR BODY WEIGHT: _____
- STEP #2: CONVERT YOUR BODY WEIGHT INTO Kg (weight ÷ 2.2 = Kg): _____
- STEP #3: Kg x RDA by group number located in "activity chart #1";
  = grams of proteins / day: _____

LIFE STYLE GROUP / 60 minutes – 90 minute fitness routine	Recommended Daily Allowance (RDA'S) by group per week
Most Adults (sedentary)	.8
Non-Vegetarian Endurance (workout or fitness)	1.2 - 1.4 = (3 - 4 days = 1.2 / 5 - 6 days = 1.3 7 days = 1.4)
Vegetarian Endurance (workout or fitness)	1.3 - 1.5 = (3-4 days = 1.3 / 5 - 6 days = 1.4 7 days = 1.5)
Non-Vegetarian Strength (weight workouts)	1.6 -1.7 = (3-4 days = 1.6 / 5-7 days = 1.7)
Vegetarian Strength (weight workout/fitness)	1.7 - 1.8 = (3-4 days = 1.7 / 5-7 days = 1.8)

Determine the percentage of calories from proteins carbohydrates, and fats = # grams of proteins carbohydrates, and fats per serving x calories per gram of proteins carbohydrates, and fats; divided by the total calories per serving. Then, multiply by 100 to get the percentage.
This = percent of calories from proteins carbohydrates, and fats per serving.

Breakfast Bar	**Servings per box 2**
Calories per serving	214
Total fat	6 grams
Total saturated fat	1.5 grams
Cholesterol	0 mg
Sodium	286 mg
Total carbs	36 grams
Dietary fiber	8 grams
Sugars	9 grams
Protein	4 grams

- **If there are 9 calories in every 1 grams of fat**
- **If there are 4 calories in every 1 gram of carbohydrates**
- **If there are 4 calories in every 1 gram of proteins**

EXAMPLE #1: Find the percentage (%) of calories from proteins carbohydrates, and fats

- Find the % of calories from protein:
  (3 grams proteins x 4 calories per gram proteins) / 167caloies x 100 = 7%,

- Find the % of calories from carbohydrates:
  (32 grams carbohydrates x 4 calories per gram carbohydrates) / 167 calories x 100 = 77%

- Find the % of calories from fat:
  (3 grams fat x 9 calories per gram fat) / 167 calories x 100 = 16%

Example #2: Find the number of calories from sugar and the percentage (%) of calories from sugar:

- 11g sugar x 4 calories per gram of sugar) = 44 calories from sugar
  44 calories of sugar / 167 calories x 100 = 26 % calories from sugar per serving

Example #3: Find the number of grams proteins, carbohydrates, or protein wanted per day =
The number of calories you eat per day x the percentage of proteins, carbohydrates, or fats wanted per day), divided by number of calories per gram of proteins, carbohydrates, or fats.

Find the number of protein grams wanted per day:

Let's use the following activity levels for men and women's protein consumption.

LIFE STYLE GROUP / 60 minutes – 90-minute fitness routine	ACTIVITY NUMBER / DAYS PER WEEK
SEDENTARY	.8 (none or limited fitness)
BEGINNER / INTERMEDIATE / fitness level	1.0 - 1.3 = (1.0 = 2 days / 1.1 = 3 days/ 1.2 = 4 days 1.3 = 5 days
ADVANCED / athlete / bodybuilder / competition	1.4 - 1.8 = (1.4 = 4 days/ 1.5 - 1.6 = 5 days/ 1.7- 1.8 = 6 - 7 days

- **SEDENTARY LIFESTYLE** = Use the activity number .8 or lower if you're in good health and sedentary.

- **ACTIVITY CATEGORY USE ACTIVITY LEVEL NUMBERS** = 1.0 – 1.3 = ACTIVE WORKOUTS for 3,4,5,6, and 7 goes up with the number of days in the week exercised.

- **MEN & WOMEN BODYBUILDERS USE ACTIVITY LEVEL NUMBERS** = 1.4 – 1.8 and at times can be much higher with the guidance of a physician / doctor. Example: Calculate 30 % of my diet coming from proteins.

How do I calculate my protein percentage per day?

- (1500 calories per day x .22 percent of proteins per day) / 4 calories per gram of proteins = 82.5 grams of protein needed each day

- (2,850 calories per day x .35 percent of proteins per day) / 4 calories per gram of proteins = 249.4 grams of protein needed each day.

How do I calculate my carbohydrate percentage per day?

- (1,650 calories per day x .65 percent of carbohydrates per day) / 4 calories per gram carbohydrates = 268.13 grams of carbohydrates per day.

- (1,865 calories per day x .55 percent of carbohydrates) / 4 calories per gram carbohydrates = 256.4 grams carbs per day.

How do I calculate my fat percentage per day?

- (2,500 calories per day x .10 percent of calories from fat per day) / 9 calories per gram of fat = 27.8 grams of fat per day.

- (2,000 calories per day x .25 percent of calories from fat per day) / 9 calories per gram of fat = 55.6 grams of fat per day.

- (2,000 calories per day x .15 percent of calories from fat) / 9 calories per gram of fat = 33.3 grams of fat per day.

CARBOHYDRATES

Carbohydrates supply us with the energy needed to sustain normal daily activity. The human body metabolizes carbohydrates faster and more efficiently than protein. There are two major types of carbohydrates, simple and complex. Simple carbohydrates or simple sugars are best represented by the monosaccharides, glucose and fructose. These simple sugars are found primarily in fruits and vegetables. Two single sugars that are combined, such as sucrose, are referred to as a disaccharide. Complex carbohydrates are best represented by three main types called starches, glycogen, and fiber. Starches from flours, bread, pasta, rice, corn, oats, barley, potatoes, and related foods make up the majority of complex carbohydrates. Glycogen is broken down into glucose when the body needs a sudden burst of energy.

Fiber, often called "bulk" or "roughage," is the indigestible portion of plant foods that helps move foods through the digestive system, delays absorption of cholesterol (and other nutrients), and softens stools by absorbing water. Dietary fiber is the non-digestible parts of plants. Functional fiber consists of non-digestible forms of carbohydrates. Even though many studies support the benefits of whole grains and high-fiber diets, the intake amongst the general public is low. We should increase our intake of dietary fiber by eating fewer refined or processed carbohydrates in favor of more whole grains, fruits, vegetables, legumes, nuts, and seeds. We eat too many refined carbohydrates which causes a high intake of added sugars.

Carbohydrates and Weight Gain

A glycemic and obesity study summarized that many high carbohydrate and low-fat diets may be counterproductive for weight control because they increase blood sugars after eating a big meal and increase excess levels of insulin. In contrast, diets that are based on low-fat foods and produce a low glycemic response (low-glycemic index foods) can assist in controlling your weight. Furthermore, this combination of low-fat and low-glycemic index foods helps balance insulin sensitivity, promotes gratification, and minimizes secretions of blood sugars following a meal (see most desired and least desired food chart). This hypothesis is supported by several intervention studies in humans in which energy-restricted diets based on low-glycemic index foods produced greater weight loss than did equivalent diets based on high-GI foods. In addition, studies also suggest that a high carbohydrate diet with a high glycemic response alters energy and appetite creating body fat.

Spikes in Blood Sugar Levels from Carbohydrates

Spikes in blood sugar levels are defined as how rapid carbohydrates are digested and released as sugars (glucose) into the bloodstream. The 2014 the American Diabetes Association's "Standards of Medical Care in Diabetes", noted that monitoring carbohydrate intake remains a key strategy in achieving glycemic control. This means that we can lower the sugars in our meals by choosing carbohydrate foods that have low to medium sugar spikes (see The Most Desired and Least Desired Food chart page 32 and glycemic info page 29). Simply remember which carbohydrates contain high sugars versus low sugars to help blood sugar levels stay balanced.

GLYCEMIC INDEX and GLYCEMIC LOAD

What is the Glycemic Index (GI)?

The glycemic index (GI) is one of the best tools for fat loss. It measures how quickly foods break down into sugar in your bloodstream. For example, potatoes have such a high GI rating that consuming them is similar to eating table sugar. In this day of "fast food" dining, you may have noticed how soon after eating you feel hungry again or fatigued. Most fast foods tend to be high on the GI, thus, your blood sugar levels spike quickly, but fall just as rapidly. Use the GI to make sure you are eating foods that absorb slower therefore resulting in less of a need for fuel throughout the day.

- **What Does the Glycemic Index (GI) Do for Us?**

    ✓ Low GI means a smaller rise in blood sugar thus helping to control diabetes.
    ✓ Low GI diets can help to lose weight while lowering blood lipids.
    ✓ Low GI diets can improve the body's sensitivity to insulin.
    ✓ High GI foods can help re-fuel carbohydrate stores after exercise.
    ✓ Brings us into a lower diet category.
    ✓ Awareness to eat breakfast cereals based on wheat bran, barley, and oats.
    ✓ Awareness of eating "grainy" bread made with whole seeds.
    ✓ Awareness to eat pasta and rice in place of potatoes.
    ✓ Awareness of using vinegar and lemon juice dressings.

What is the Glycemic Load (GL)?

The glycemic load measures the amount of carbohydrates in each serving of food. Foods with a glycemic load under ten are good choices because these foods should be your first choice when choosing your carbohydrates at mealtime. Foods between 10 to 20 on the glycemic load scale have a moderate effect on your blood sugars. Carbohydrates with glycemic loads greater than 20 on the scale will cause sugars in your blood to spike. Lowering your glycemic load has been shown to make a difference in blood glucose levels, weight control, and prevention of heart disease. Best of all, the benefits you reap can help you feel good and have more energy to do the things you enjoy.

Calculating Glycemic Load:

- To find a food's GL, multiply its GI by the number of carbohydrate grams in a serving, and then divide by 100. A low GL is between 1 and 10; a moderate GL is 11 to 19, and a high GL is 20 or higher. For those with diabetes, you want your diet to have GL values as low as possible.

Glycemic Load Points

Glycemic load values help you assess how food portions affect blood sugar levels. Glycemic load is a measure that takes into account the amount of carbohydrate in a portion of food together with how quickly it raises blood glucose levels.

Glycemic Load = GI x Carbohydrate (g) content per portion ÷ 100
Using an apple as an example: GI value = 38; Carbohydrate per serve = 15g

- GL = $\frac{38 \times 15}{\text{divided by 100}}$

- = GL = 5.7

The GL of a typical apple is 6

Similar to the glycemic index, the glycemic load of a food can be classified as low, medium, or high:

Low: 10 <=
Medium: 11 – 19
High: 20 =>

GLYCEMIC LOAD (*Sugar Load Points*) PER DAY VS WEIGHT

- 0 – 150 LBS = 55 POINTS
- 151 – 175 LBS = 65 POINTS
- 176 LBS – ABOVE= 80 POINTS

The Importance of the Glycemic Index and Glycemic Load

The goal is to have some knowledge about the glycemic index so that you can minimize your hunger and lessen the tendency to "cheat" or overeat. As a result, you can continue to lose body fat or maintain your weight. Foods that are low on the GI will also help eliminate mood swings and regulate energy levels. We don't want foods that stimulate insulin surges which causes people to eat 60 - 70% more calories later in the day. Studies have concluded that individuals who consume foods high in glucose such as white bread, commercial whole wheat bread, and raisins eat an average of 200 calories more at the next meal than those who eat fructose (a sugar found in fruits). Foods low on the GI scale can be mixed with modest quantities of high glycemic foods without losing their hunger-reducing effect. The purpose of the scale is not to have you eliminate less nutritious choices from your diet, but rather balance the foods that are "less desirable" by eating them with foods that are "most or moderately desirable" (see chart page 32).

Low Glycemic Food Plan

Pro's	Con's
Helps with Diabetes, Hypoglycemia, Insulin Resistance, Syndrome X	Elevates Insulin and Blood Glucose
Greater weight loss for dieters	Stimulates fat-storage
Reduces excess body fat	Exacerbates hyperactivity
Increases sports performance for athletes	Reduces Sports Performance

Low glycemic food plans are not based on starvation or deprivation. Eating is a part of our lives and we should not have to sacrifice tasty foods to stay healthy. These plans focus on reducing the ingestion of foods that elevate insulin and stimulate fat-storage. We cannot entirely eliminate high glycemic foods from our diet, but we can be more aware of the glycemic reaction that foods have and make better choices. Other benefits applied to a low GI food plan are reduced incidences of Type II diabetes while helping control Type I and II diabetes, hypoglycemia, and hypertension.

THE MOST DESIRED vs LEAST DESIRED GLYCEMIC FOODS

	Most Desired Foods	Moderately Desired	Least Desired
Breads	Whole Grain, Wheat, Rye Pita Bread, Cracked, Sprouted Whole Wheat	100% Stone Ground Whole Wheat, Pumpernickel, 100% Whole Grain Rye Crisp Cracker	White bread, most commercial whole wheat breads, English muffins, bagel, French bread, most commercial matzo
Cereals:	Bran cereals (All-Bran, Fiber One) Coarse Oatmeal, Porridge, Coarse Whole Grain (Kashi) Cereal mixed with Psyllium (Fiber wise)	Grape-nut cereal, medium-fine grain oatmeal	Corn flakes, puffed rice, puffed wheat, flaked cereals, instant "Quick" or pre-cooked cereals: oat bran, rolled oats, shredded wheat, Muesli.
Fruit	Most fruit and natural fruit juices, including apple, berries, cantaloupe, grapefruit, honeydew, oranges, pears, grapes, peaches, applesauce, (Cherries, plums, and grapefruit lowest)	Banana, Kiwi, Mango, papaya, orange juice.	Pineapple, raisins, watermelon, fruit juices sweetened with sugar.
Milk Products	Skim milk, 1% milk, cottage cheese, (low-fat or regular), Buttermilk, Low-fat plain yogurt, Low-fat fruited yogurt, Low-fat frozen yogurt (artificial sweetener)	2% milk, cheese, regular plain yogurt	Whole milk, ice milk, ice cream, yogurt sweetened with sugar, low-fat frozen desserts with sugar added, low-fat and regular frozen yogurt with sugar added, tofu ice cream
Meat	Shellfish, "white" fish (cod, flounder, trout, tuna in water), chicken, turkey, Cornish hen, venison (white meat no skin), egg substitutes (cholesterol free), cottage cheese	Higher fat fish (salmon, herring), lean cuts of beef, pork, veal, low-fat imitation luncheon meat, low-fat cheese, eggs.	Most cuts of beef, pork, lamb, hot dogs (including "low-fat' versions), cheese, lunch meats, peanut butter
Pasta, Grains, and Starchy Vegetables	Pasta (all types), barley, bulgur, buckwheat (kasha) couscous, kidney beans dry, lentils, black-eyed peas, chick-peas, kidney beans, lima beans, peas, sweet potato, yams, soybeans (lowest), Most Vegetables.	Rice, boiled potato, corn, navy beans, kidney beans (canned), baked beans, beets	Instant rice, brown rice, instant precooked grains, baked potato, micro-waved potato, instant potato, winter squash (acorn, butternut), carrots, parsnips

FATS

There are 9 calories in every 1 gram of fat.

Fats help promote a healthy cell function and play a vital role in healthy hair, skin, maintaining temperature, and insulating organs. In our diet, they are the most energy dense source of calories. Consumption of fats in moderation is essential to health, but overconsumption can lead to cardiovascular disease and weight gain.

The 2 Categories of Fats

Saturated Fats - Fats that come from animal sources and become solid at room temperature.

Unsaturated Fats - Fats that come from plants sources and are liquid at room temperature. They include most vegetable oils.

KEY HEALTH RECOMMENDATIONS

For reference, see chart THE MOST DESIRED vs LEAST DESIRED GLYCEMIC FOODS
- Watch salad dressings, use more low calorie and vinaigrettes
- Use soy, olive, peanut, and canola oils instead of lard and butter
- Add fruits and vegetables
- Add walnuts, walnut oil, ground flaxseed, green leafy vegetables into your diet
- Choose fish, lean cuts of meats, skinless poultry
- Focus on nonfat and low-fat dairy products
- Use substitutes for butter, margarine, oils, sour cream, mayonnaise, and full-fat
- Use less or avoid organ meats, cold cuts, all hot dogs (processed), sausages, and bacon
- Use less or avoid margarine products with trans fatty acids
- Avoid creams and white sauces
- Make protein the focus of each meal as it kicks your metabolism into higher gear. Fish and poultry are the real "guilt-free" foods. The advantages of a protein meal will help in maintaining insulin levels, building muscle, and repairing tissue. All which are essential for preventing diabetes and staying lean.
- Eat a high protein breakfast every morning. It will stabilize your blood sugar and get you off to a good start.
- Avoid least desired grains
- Choose low glycemic vegetables
- Choose berries and fruits you can eat with the skin
- Avoid white flour foods, potatoes, sugar, and salt
- Snack on seeds and nuts, they have Omega 3's and are full of protein
- Avoid too much: caffeine, processed foods, foods with high fructose corn syrup, and trans fatty foods as they increase insulin resistance.

The Importance of Eating Grains

Whole grain is defined as foods that contain the entire grain. Consuming foods containing fiber, such as whole grains, as part of a healthy diet may reduce the risk of heart disease and constipation. Eating whole grains may also assist with weight management. Foods that contain whole grains are brown rice, wild rice, buckwheat, triticale, bulgur (cracked wheat), millet, quinoa, sorghum, whole wheat, oats/oatmeal, rye, barley, corn, and popcorn.

For a 2,000-calorie diet, the USDA recommends a total of 6-ounces of grains each day. One ounce is about a slice of bread or 1/2 cup of rice or pasta. Below are examples of whole grain serving sizes, each count as 1 ounce-equivalent (or 1 serving) of whole grains:

- 1 slice whole-grain bread (such as 100% whole-wheat bread)
- 1 cup ready-to-eat, whole-grain cereal
- ½ cup cooked whole-grain cereal, brown rice, or whole-wheat pasta
- 5 whole-grain crackers
- 3 cups unsalted, air-popped popcorn
- 16-inch whole-wheat tortilla.

HELPFUL GUIDELINES FOR FRUITS / VEGETABLES FOR THE DAY

Very Active 5-7 days a week: An average of 60 minutes of exercise or more a day.

- Men ages 19-30: 2 1/2 cups Fruits + 4 cups Veggies = 6 1/2 cups TOTAL
- Women ages 19-50: 2 cups Fruits + 3 cups Veggies = 5 cups TOTAL
- Men ages 31-50: 2 1/2 cups + 3 1/2 cups Veggies = 6 cups TOTAL
- Women ages 51+: 2 cups Fruits + 2 1/2 cups Veggies = 4 1/2 cups TOTAL
- Men ages 51+: 2 cups Fruits + 3 cups Veggies = 5 cups TOTAL

Moderately Active 3-4 days a week: An average of 30 to 60 minutes of exercise a day.

- Women ages 19-50: 2 cups Fruits + 2 1/2 cups Veggies = 4 1/2 cups TOTAL
- Men ages 19-30: 2 cups Fruits + 3 1/2 cups Veggies = 5 1/2 cups TOTAL
- Women ages 51+: 1 1/2 cups Fruits + 2 1/2 cups Veggies = 4 cups TOTAL
- Men ages 31+: 2 cups Fruits + 3 cups Veggies = 5 cups TOTAL

Lightly Active: An average of less than 30 minutes of exercise a day.

- Women ages 19-30: 2 cups Fruits + 2 1/2 cups Veggies = 4 1/2 cups TOTAL
- Men ages 19-50: 2 cups Fruits + 3 cups Veggies = 5 cups TOTAL
- Women ages 31-50: 1 1/2 cups Fruits + 2 1/2 cups Veggies = 4 cups TOTAL
- Men ages 51+: 2 cups Fruits + 2 1/2 cups Veggies = 4 1/2 cups TOTAL
- Women ages 51+: 1 1/2 cups Fruits + 2 cups Veggies = 3 1/2 cups TOTAL

	Recommended Ranges (Percent of Calories)	Lower Carb Higher Protein (Percent of Calories)
Carbohydrates	45-65%	25-30%
Protein	10-35%	45-40%
Fat	20-35%	30%

HOW DO I CALCULATE THE USA RECOMMENDED DAILY ALLOWANCE FOR PROTEINS (USA RDA)?

LIFE STYLE GROUP / 60 minutes – 90-minute fitness routine	Recommended Daily Allowance (RDA'S) by group per week
Most Adults (sedentary)	.8
Non-Vegetarian Endurance (workout or fitness)	1.2 - 1.4 = (3 - 4 days = 1.2 / 5 - 6 days = 1.3 7 days = 1.4)
Vegetarian Endurance (workout or fitness)	1.3 - 1.5 = (3-4 days = 1.3 / 5 - 6 days = 1.4 7 days = 1.5)
Non-Vegetarian Strength (weight workouts)	1.6 -1.7 = (3-4 days = 1.6 / 5-7 days = 1.7)
Vegetarian Strength (weight workout/fitness)	1.7 - 1.8 = (3-4 days = 1.7 / 5-7 days = 1.8)

THE F.I.T.T. PRINCIPLE

THE F.I.T.T PRINCIPLE is a formula that monitors an exercise/fitness program at all levels. The acronym FITT represents Frequency, Intensity, Time, and Type. Although the F.I.T.T. principle is commonly used in the weight loss industry, it can also be a part of strength and conditioning programs. The F.I.T.T. principle charts are located on page 38-39.

- **Frequency** is defined as the how often you exercise (day, weekly, monthly, etc.)
- **Intensity** is defined as how hard you exercise
- **Time** is defined as refers to the time how long you exercise
- **Type** is defined as what kind of exercise is performed

F.I.T.T. Principle Basic Recommendation for Results

- **Frequency** – 5 to 6 times per week
- **Intensity** – raising the heart rate rises in a training zone (beats per mins) during exercise
- **Time** – 60-90 minutes
- **Type** – The exercise choices used for the workout routine may include cardiovascular, muscular endurance, muscular strength, or flexibility exercises. The type can include all types at once using a circuit or cross fit routine.

A BETTER UNDERSTANDING OF CARDIOVASCULAR EXERCISE

Definitions:
- **Maximum Heart Rate (MHR)** = 220 – age
- **Target Heart Rate (THR):** A heart rate that is reached during aerobic exercise that represents the minimum level of exertion at which cardiovascular fitness can increase for an individual at any given age group. THR is usually a pre-determined pulse rate to target during aerobic (ex: 60%)
- **Target Heart Rate Zone (THZ):** An estimated range of how fast your heart should beat during exercise. It should be a safe but effective range for a specific workout.
  - ✓ A quick way to measure the training heart rate is by taking the pulse for 6 seconds. Add a zero to the number of beats from the pulse = 70 bpm (example: if the pulse rate is 7 for 6 seconds, add a 0 to the pulse rate but for the best and most accurate results use a heart rate monitor).

Intensity and The F.I.T.T. Principle

- **STEP 1 - Maximum Heart Rate (MHR):** If Jane is 20 years old what is her maximum heart rate (MHR): 220 – 20 = MHR for Jane is 200.

- **STEP 2 - Target Heart Rate (THR):** Joey is 40 years old. He has decided to put forth a 100% effort in losing his weight with a good exercise routine and a fun-filled diet (no fad diets; he is watching his glycemic index and his caloric intake). Since Joey weighs 600 pounds, Dr. Sims has started him on an exercise routine for the first 3 months that involves walking for 20-30 minutes per day 6 days per week (walk around the corner, treadmill, or at the local college or high school track). Dr. Sims gave Joey a target heart rate of 60%. To make this an easy fitness journey, Joey purchased a heart monitor for the next 3-months to assist him in tracking his target heart rate. After 3-months Joey has reduced his weight from 600 to 546 pounds. Now that Joey feels comfortable about his exercise routine, Dr. Sims has suggested that Joey use a training heart rate zone. This type of zone allows Joey to speed up his heart rate (higher beats per min = bpm) while exercising. Also, the heart rate training zone will allow Joey the freedom to slow down his heart rate (lower bpm) at any time. Using the target heart rate zone allows Joey to walk a little faster, yet slow down to catch his breath at any time.

Joey Example: *(note, when using percentages in math the decimal point must be moved to the left two places)*

Equation for Target Heart Rate (THR)

- MHR = 220 – 40 = 180
- THR = MHR x 60% (note, 60% = 0.60, Joey's Doctor informed him to target 60%)
- THR = 180 x .60 = 108 beats per minute

Equation for Target Heart Rate Zone (THZ)

- THZ = MHR x two percentages to create a low and a high area (zone) for your heart rate (bpm) during the entire exercise routine
- MHR = 220 – 40 = 180
- 1st Zone (60%):
  - ✓ THR = 180 x .60 = 108 beats per minute
- 2nd Zone (80%):
  - ✓ THR = 180 x .80 = 144 beats per minute
- THZ = 108 and 144 beats per minute.
- Along with understanding the glycemic index and calorie counting, the target heart rate zone is the healthiest way to shed pounds quickly.

F.I.T.T. Principle for Cardiovascular

The purpose of the cardiovascular program is to promote weight loss and body tone by keeping the heart rate training zone between 60% and 100%, 6-days per week in conjunction with a good nutrition plan. Use variety when selecting cardiovascular exercises.

CHART 1 - F.I.T.T Principle for a Cardiovascular Program

F Frequency	Tuesday	Wednesday	Thursday	Friday	Sunday
I Intensity	HR: 50-80%	HR: 70-100%	HR: 60-90%	HR: 55-85%	HR: 65-95%
	101-161.6	141.4-202	121.2-181.8	111.1-171.7	131.3-191.9
T Time	65 min	90 min	60 min	75 min	85 min
T Type	65 min Stairs	90 min Run & Jog	60 min Zumba	10 min High Knees 20 min Stairs 45 min Power Walk	45 min Bike 40 min Elliptical

WEEKLY FITNESS ROUTINE USING THE FITT PRINCIPLE IN A 5-7 DAY ROUTINE:
Use continuous movement using flexibility, cardiovascular exercise, and muscular endurance = WEIGHT LOSS.

Purpose Weight Loss: Creating weight loss and body tone by keeping the heart rate training zone between 60% and 100%, 6-days a week and using a sound nutritional plan.

CHART 2 - F.I.T.T. Principle Cardiovascular Weight Loss Routine

Stretch	10 min Stretch		10 min Stretch	10 min Stretch	15 min Stretch	Optional Stretch
F Frequency	Monday	Tuesday	Wednesday	Thursday	Friday	Saturday
I Intensity	60-100 %	60-100 %	60-100 %	60-100 %	60-100 %	60-100 %
	MHR – age x each % = zone	MHR – age x each % = zone	MHR – age x each % = zone	MHR – age x each % = zone	MHR – age x each % = zone	MHR – age x each % = zone
T Time	40 min cardio / 20 mins weights / 20 min core	90 mins	60 mins / 15 min circuit + 15 min core	60 mins cardio / 20 mins weights	60-90 mins all cardio	Mandatory all cardio for 90 mins
T Type	Cardio / weights / core	All cardio	Cardio / core	Cardio / weights	All cardio	All cardio

Purpose of Muscular Endurance: Creating body tone by keeping the heart rate training zone between 75% and 100%, 5 to 6-days a week and using a sound nutritional plan.

CHART 3 - F.I.T.T Principle for a Muscular Endurance Program

F Frequency	Mondays	Tuesday	Wednesday	Saturday	Sunday
I Intensity	50-70%	46-74%	45-73%	51-75%	48-72%
	101-141.4	92.92-149.48	90.9-147.46	103.02-151.5	96.96-145.44
T Time	45 min	75 min	50 min	70 min	45 min
T Type	Lower Body 15 Circuit Stations	Upper Body 5 Circuit Stations	Full Body 25 Circuit Stations	Upper Body 10 Circuit Stations	Lower Body 10 Circuit Stations

F.I.T.T Principle for a Strength Program

*Energy in (food) must be "greater" than the Energy Out (burned) = "WEIGHT GAINED"

For maximum results using the strength training F.I.T.T. principle chart, the athlete should consume more energy in (food) than energy out (burned) (see meal plan example in nutrition section).

CHART 4 - F.I.T.T Principle for a Strength Program

F Frequency	Wednesday	Thursday	Friday	Saturday	Sunday
I Intensity	50-80%	60-90%	55-85%	70-100%	65-95%
	101-161.16	121.12-181.8	111.1-171.7	141.4-202	131.3-191.9
T Time	60 min	45 min	60 min	45 min	60 min
T Type	Front Quads 8 Sets / 5 Reps -Biceps 4 Sets / 5 Reps	Chest 8 Sets / 5 Reps - Military Press 4 Sets / 5 Reps	Power Cleans 8 Sets / 5 Reps Hamstrings 4 Sets /5 Reps	-Back 8 Sets / 5 Reps -Shoulders 4 Sets	Deadlift 8 Sets / 5 Reps Triceps 4 Sets / 5 Reps

EXERCISE ZONES USING INTENSITY CALCULATIONS

EXERCISE ZONES

EFFORT	AGE	20	25	30	35	40	45	50	55	65	70
	100%	200	195	190	185	180	175	170	165	155	150
		Maximum Effort Zone									
	90%	180	176	171	167	162	158	153	149	140	135
		Anaerobic Zone									
	80%	160	156	152	148	144	140	136	132	124	120
		Aerobic Zone									
	70%	140	137	133	130	126	123	119	116	109	105
		Weight Control Zone									
	60%	120	117	114	111	108	105	102	99	93	90
		Moderate Activity									
	50%	100	98	95	93	90	88	85	83	78	75
		Warm Up Zone									

MEASUREMENTS AND ASSESSMENTS CHARTS

NAME: _____   SCORE: _____ / _____

MHR = 220 – age = _____ / THZ = MHR x Low _____ % & MHR x High _____ %

TESTING WEEK

CARDIOVASCULAR, FLEXIBITY, & MUSCLE ENDURANCE 1

1a. Record Resting Heart Rate = _____

1b. 3-Minute Step Test: Record heart rate after step test is complete = _____

1c. Record how many minutes it takes the heart to return to the starting resting heart rate number (see 1a)? Total time: _____

2. Flexibility / Sit & Reach Test
Inches before toes: _____ / Inches past toes: _____

3a. Machine circuit training: 4 sets of 6 stations @ 12 Reps
How many full circuits were completed? _____
How much time was used to complete this assessment? _____

3b. Free weight circuit training: 4 sets of 6 stations @ 10 Reps
How many full circuits were completed? _____
How much time was used to complete this assessment? _____

4. 1st: 1 Mile - Run / Jog / Power Walk
                Final Time: _____

5. Machine Chest / Vertical Press or Free Weight Bench Press
    Machine: Women: 25lbs / Men: 75lbs: How many total reps in 60 secs: _____
    Free Weight: Women: 45lbs bar / Men: 135lbs: How many total reps in 60 secs: _____

6. ½ mile run: Record your time: _____

7. 6-minute stadium stair run / How many totals rows of stairs completed? _____

NAME: _____   **SCORE:** _____ / _____

MHR = 220 – age = _____   / THZ = MHR x Low _____ % & MHR x High _____ %

TESTING WEEK

BODY COMPOSITION, CARDIOVASUCALR, MUSCLE ENDURANCE - 1

MEN: BODY COMPOSITION MEASUREMENT
1a. Bodyweight : _____
1b. Waist Measurement : _____
1c. MEN: Body Fat Measurement : _____

EQ 1: (1.082 x your total weight in pounds) - (4.15 x your waist measurement in inches) + 94.42 = equals male "lean body weight".

EQ 2: (original body weight - lean body weight) ÷ original body weight = this "answer" x 100 = male "body fat percentage".

1d. What's your final lean body weight? _____
1e. What's your final body fat percentage? _____

WOMEN: BODY COMPOSITION MEASUREMENT
2a. Body Weight = _____
2b. Waist Measurement = _____
2c. Hips Measurement = _____
2d. Forearm Measurement = _____
2e. Wrist Measurement = _____

EQ 1: (0.732 x body weight) - (0.157 x waist measurement) – (0.249 x hip measurement) + (0.434 x forearm measurement) + (wrist measurement ÷ 3.14) + 8.987 = equals woman's "lean body weight".

EQ 2: (Body Weight - Lean Body Weight) ÷ Body Weight = ANSWER, then multiply answer by 100 for a percentage = woman "body fat percentage".

2f. What's your final lean body weight? _____
2g. What's your final body fat percentage? _____

3. Cardiovascular Endurance "Jump Rope"
How many times did you skip rope in 90 secs (1 jump + rope turn): _____?

4. Muscular Endurance
4a. Push- Ups: How many in 60 secs: = _____

4b. V- Ups: How many in 60 secs: = _____

4c. Women - Squats with 10lbs / How many in 60 secs = _____

4d. Men - Squats with 45lbs / How many in 60 secs = _____
4e. Women: Standard Pull-ups: How many in 60 SECS (body weight or machine assistance) _____
4f. Men: Standard Pull-ups: How many in 60 SECS (body weight or machine assistance) _____

NAME: _____   SCORE: _____ / _____

MHR = 220 – age = _____ / THZ = MHR x Low _____ % & MHR x High _____ %

TESTING WEEK

CARDIOVASCULAR, FLEXIBITY, & MUSCLE ENDURANCE - 2

1a. Record Resting Heart Rate = _____

1b. 3-Minute Step Test: Record heart rate after step test is complete = _____

1c. Record how many minutes it takes the heart to return to the starting resting heart rate number (see 1a)? Total time: _____

2. Flexibility / Sit & Reach Test
Inches before toes: _____ / Inches past toes: _____

3a. Machine circuit training: 4 sets of 8 stations @ 12 Reps
How many full circuits were completed? _____
How much time was used to complete this assessment? _____

3b. Free weight circuit training: 4 sets of 8 stations @ 10 Reps
How many full circuits were completed? _____
How much time was used to complete this assessment? _____

4. 1st: 1 Mile - Run / Jog / Power Walk
                    Final Time: _____

5. Machine Chest / Vertical Press or Free Weight Bench Press
    Machine: Women: 25lbs / Men: 75lbs: How many total reps in 60 secs: _____
    Free Weight: Women: 45lbs bar / Men: 135lbs: How many total reps in 60 secs: _____

6. ½ mile run: Record your time: _____

7. 6-minute stadium stair run / How many totals rows of stairs completed? _____

NAME: _____   **SCORE:** _____ / _____

MHR = 220 – age = _____ **/ THZ = MHR x Low** _____ **% & MHR x High** _____ **%**

TESTING WEEK -

BODY COMPOSITION, CARDIOVASUCALR, MUSCLE ENDURANCE - 2

MEN: BODY COMPOSITION MEASUREMENT
1a. Bodyweight: _____
1b. Waist Measurement: _____
1c. MEN: Body Fat Measurement: _____
EQ 1: (1.082 x your total weight in pounds) - (4.15 x your waist measurement in inches) + 94.42 = equals male "lean body weight":
EQ 2: (original body weight - lean body weight) ÷ original body weight = this "answer" x 100 = men "body fat percentage".

1d. What's your final lean body weight? _____
1e. What's your final body fat percentage? _____

WOMEN: BODY COMPOSITION MEASUREMENT
2a. Body Weight = _____
2b. Waist Measurement = _____
2c. Hips Measurement = _____
2d. Forearm Measurement = _____
2e. Wrist Measurement = _____

EQ 1: (0.732 x body weight) - (0.157 x waist measurement) – (0.249 x hip measurement) + (0.434 x forearm measurement) + (wrist measurement ÷ 3.14) + 8.987 = equals woman's "lean body weight".

EQ 2: (Body Weight - Lean Body Weight) ÷ Body Weight = ANSWER, then multiply answer by 100 for a percentage = woman "body fat percentage".

2f. What's your final lean body weight? _____
2g. What's your final body fat percentage? _____

3. Cardiovascular Endurance "Jump Rope"
How many times did you skip rope in 90 secs (1 jump + rope turn): _____?

4. Muscular Endurance
4a. Push- Ups: How many in 60 secs: = _____

4b. V- Ups: How many in 60 secs: = _____

4c. Women - Squats with 10lbs / How many in 60 secs = _____

4d. Men - Squats with 45lbs / How many in 60 secs = _____
4e. Women: Standard Pull-ups: How many in 60 SECS (body weight or machine assistance) _____
4f. Men: Standard Pull-ups: How many in 60 SECS (body weight or machine assistance) _____

NAME: _____   **SCORE:** _____ / _____

MHR = 220 – age = _____ / THZ = MHR x Low _____ % & MHR x High _____ %

TESTING WEEK

CARDIOVASCULAR, FLEXIBITY, & MUSCLE ENDURANCE - 3

1a. Record Resting Heart Rate = _____

1b. 3-Minute Step Test: Record heart rate after step is complete = _____

1c. Record how many minutes it takes the heart to return to the starting resting heart rate number (see 1a)?   Total time: _____

2. Flexibility / Sit & Reach Test
Inches before toes: _____/ Inches past toes: _____

3a. Machine circuit training: 4 sets of 10 stations @ 12 Reps
How many full circuits were completed? _____
How much time was used to complete this assessment? _____

3b. Free weight circuit training: 4 sets of 10 stations @ 10 Reps
How many full circuits were completed? _____
How much time was used to complete this assessment? _____

4. 1st: 1 Mile - Run / Jog / Power Walk
                          Final Time: _____

5. Machine Chest / Vertical Press or Free Weight Bench Press
    Machine: Women: 25lbs / Men: 75lbs: How many total reps in 60 secs: _____
    Free Weight: Women: 45lbs bar / Men: 135lbs: How many total reps in 60 secs: _____

6. ½ mile run: Record your time: _____

7. 6-minute stadium stair run / How many totals rows of stairs completed? _____

NAME: _____   SCORE: _____ / _____

MHR = 220 – age = _____ / THZ = MHR x Low _____ % & MHR x High _____ %

TESTING WEEK

BODY COMPOSITION, CARDIOVASUCALR, MUSCLE ENDURANCE - 3

MEN: BODY COMPOSITION MEASUREMENT #3
1a. Bodyweight: _____
1b. Waist Measurement: _____
1c. MEN: Body Fat Measurement: _____
EQ 1: (1.082 x your total weight in pounds) - (4.15 x your waist measurement in inches) + 94.42 = equals male "lean body weight":

EQ 2: (original body weight - lean body weight) ÷ original body weight = this "answer" x 100 = men "body fat percentage".

1d. What's your final lean body weight? _____
1e. What's your final body fat percentage? _____

WOMEN: BODY COMPOSITION MEASUREMENT
2a. Body Weight = _____
2b. Waist Measurement = _____
2c. Hips Measurement = _____
2d. Forearm Measurement = _____
2e. Wrist Measurement = _____

EQ 1: (0.732 x body weight) - (0.157 x waist measurement) – (0.249 x hip measurement) + (0.434 x forearm measurement) + (wrist measurement ÷ 3.14) + 8.987 = equals woman's "lean body weight".

EQ 2: (Body Weight - Lean Body Weight) ÷ Body Weight = ANSWER, then multiply answer by 100 for a percentage = woman "body fat percentage".

2f. What's your final lean body weight? _____
2g. What's your final body fat percentage? _____

3. Cardiovascular Endurance "Jump Rope"
How many times did you skip rope in 90 secs (1 jump + rope turn): _____?

4. Muscular Endurance
4a. Push- Ups: How many in 60 secs: = _____

4b. V- Ups: How many in 60 secs: = _____

4c. Women - Squats with 10lbs / How many in 60 secs = _____

4d. Men - Squats with 45lbs / How many in 60 secs = _____
4e. Women: Standard Pull-ups: How many in 60 SECS (body weight or machine assistance) _____
4f. Men: Standard Pull-ups: How many in 60 SECS (body weight or machine assistance) _____

NAME: _____   SCORE: _____ / _____

MHR = 220 – age = _____ / THZ = MHR x Low _____ % & MHR x High _____ %

FINAL TESTING WEEK: DAY #1

CARDIOVASCULAR, FLEXIBITY, & MUSCLE ENDURANCE - 4

1a. Record Resting Heart Rate = _____

1b. 3-Minute Step Test: Record heart rate after step is complete = _____

1c. Record how many minutes it takes the heart to return to the starting resting heart rate number (see 1a)?   Total time: _____

2. Flexibility / Sit & Reach Test
Inches before toes: _____ / Inches past toes: _____

3a. Machine circuit training: 4 sets of 12 stations @ 12 Reps
How many full circuits were completed? _____
How much time was used to complete this assessment? _____

3b. Free weight circuit training: 4 sets of 12 stations @ 10 Reps
How many full circuits were completed? _____
How much time was used to complete this assessment? _____

4. 1st: 1 Mile - Run / Jog / Power Walk
                    Final Time: _____
5. Machine Chest / Vertical Press or Free Weight Bench Press
     Machine: Women: 25lbs / Men: 75lbs: How many total reps in 60 secs: _____
     Free Weight: Women: 45lbs bar / Men: 135lbs:
     How many total reps in 60 secs? _____

6. ½ mile run: Record your time: _____

7. 6-minute stadium stair run / How many totals rows of stairs completed? _____

**FINAL WEEK: INSTRUCTOR / COACH OBSTACLE COURSE: 1 set of 8 stations:
a. 1 mile, b. 10 stations weight circuit, c. 90 sec jump rope, d. 10 – 25 push –ups, e. 25 – 50 v-ups, f. pull ups (body weight or machine assistance), g. ½ mile run, g. vertical press, h. 6-minute stadium stair run

Record Final Time: _____

NAME: _____ SCORE: _____ / _____

MHR = 220 – age = _____ / THZ = MHR x Low _____ % & MHR x High _____ %

FINAL TESTING WEEK: DAY #2

BODY COMPOSITION, CARDIOVASUCALR, MUSCLE ENDURANCE - 4

MEN: BODY COMPOSITION MEASUREMENT
1a. Bodyweight: _____
1b. Waist Measurement: _____
1c. MEN: Body Fat Measurement: _____
EQ 1: (1.082 x your total weight in pounds) - (4.15 x your waist measurement in inches) + 94.42 = equals male "lean body weight":

EQ 2: (original body weight - lean body weight) ÷ original body weight = this "answer" x 100 = men "body fat percentage".

1d. What's your final lean body weight? _____
1e. What's your final body fat percentage? _____

WOMEN: BODY COMPOSITION MEASUREMENT
2a. Body Weight = _____
2b. Waist Measurement = _____
2c. Hips Measurement = _____
2d. Forearm Measurement = _____
2e. Wrist Measurement = _____

EQ 1: (0.732 x body weight) - (0.157 x waist measurement) – (0.249 x hip measurement) + (0.434 x forearm measurement) + (wrist measurement ÷ 3.14) + 8.987 = equals woman's "lean body weight".

EQ 2: (Body Weight - Lean Body Weight) ÷ Body Weight = ANSWER, then multiply answer by 100 for a percentage = woman "body fat percentage".

2f. What's your final lean body weight? _____
2g. What's your final body fat percentage? _____

WORKBOOK ASSIGNMENTS

MEASUREMENT & ASSESSMENT #1: Blood Pressure Test (25 points)

Knowing your blood pressure measurement is crucial in our everyday life because it is related to heart disease. As your heart beats, it contracts and pushes blood through the arteries and the rest of your body. This is called the Systolic Blood Pressure (the top number). This force creates pressure on the arteries. Normal systolic blood pressure is below 120. The diastolic blood pressure number (the bottom number) indicates the pressure in the arteries when the heart rests between beats. A normal diastolic blood pressure number is less than 80.

Why is taking your blood pressure important? The American Heart Association states that knowing your blood pressure is essential to decrease the risk of health problems. If your blood pressure is high, it is putting extra strain on your arteries and heart. This extra strain can cause the arteries to become less flexible causing them to narrow. This narrowing will likely clog the artery. Taking your blood pressure once a year is ideal; however, if you have high blood pressure, consult with a physician.

Try it yourself: *(After taking blood pressure circle the grade and record the data using the chart below.)*

GRADE	acceptable	borderline	high
Systolic	< 140	140 - 160	> 160
Diastolic	< 85	85 - 95	> 95

Record Pre – Test: 1: ACCEPTABLE / BORDERLINE / HIGH
   1. Resting Heart Rate: _____
   2. Systolic: _____
   3. Diastolic: _____
   4. Pulse: _____

Record Post – Test: 2: ACCEPTABLE / BORDERLINE / HIGH
   1. Resting Heart Rate: _____
   2. Systolic: _____
   3. Diastolic: _____
   4. Pulse: _____

Record Post – Test: 3: ACCEPTABLE / BORDERLINE / HIGH
   1. Resting Heart Rate: _____
   2. Systolic: _____
   3. Diastolic: _____
   4. Pulse: _____

Record Post – Test: 4: ACCEPTABLE / BORDERLINE / HIGH
   1. Resting Heart Rate: _____
   2. Systolic: _____
   3. Diastolic: _____
   4. Pulse: _____

MEASUREMENT & ASSESSMENT #2: Body Mass / Weight (25 points):

1) Pre-weight 1: Record your weight from the class weight scale: _____
2) Post-weight 2:Record your weight from the class weight scale: _____
3) Post-weight 3: Record your weight from the class weight scale: _____
4) Post-weight 4: Record your weight from the class weight scale: _____

MEASUREMENT & ASSESSMENT #3A & #3B: Body Composition

The Skin Fold Caliper Without A Device: (100 points)

#3A: INSTRUCTIONS FOR MEN ONLY: Use examples in steps 1 & 2 below to find the lean body mass and body fat percentage for males without a skinfold caliper. For full credit record the four final answers to the questions at the end of this exercise. Measure all measurement in inches.

MALE DATA: If Joe weighs 155lbs, and has a 35-inch waist

Example
- **STEP 1: Find Joe's lean body weight:**
  - ✓ (1.082 x your total weight in pounds) - (4.15 x your waist measurement in inches) + 94.42 = this answer equals male "lean body weight."
  - ✓ **Answer: (1.082 x 155) – (4.15 x 35) + 94.42 = 116.88 lbs. = lean body weight**

- **STEP 2: Find Joe's body fat percentage.**
  - ✓ (original body weight - lean body weight) ÷ original body weight = this "answer" x 100 = male "body fat percentage."
  - ✓ **Answer: (155 – 116.88) = 38.12 ÷ 155 = .2459 x 100 = 24.59% = male body fat percentage**

MEN: COMPLETE MEASUREMENT & ASSESSMENT and RECORD FINAL INFORMATION HERE:

1. What's your weight? _____
2. What's your measured waist? _____
3. What's your lean body weight? _____
4. What's your body fat percentage? _____

#3B: INSTRUCTIONS FOR WOMEN ONLY: Use examples in steps 1 & 2 below to find the lean body mass and body fat percentage for women without a skinfold caliper. For full credit record the seven final answers to the questions at the end of this exercise. Complete all measurements in inches.

WOMEN measure the following five areas:
- W\weight in lbs.
- Waist at navel
- hips at fullest point
- forearm at fullest point
- wrist at thinnest point

FEMALE DATA: If "Cindy" weighs 143 lbs., 28" inch waist, 39" inches hip, 10" inches in forearm, 6.5" inches in wrist.

Example

- **STEP 1: Equation to find Cindy's lean body weight:**
  - ✓ (0.732 x body weight) - (0.157 x waist measurement) – (0.249 x hip measurement) + (0.434 x forearm measurement) + (wrist measurement ÷ 3.14) + 8.987
  - ✓ **Answer: (0.732 x 143lbs) - (0.157 x 28) – (0.249 x 39) + (0.434 x 10) + (6.5 ÷ 3.14) + 8.987 = 106 lbs. of lean body weight**

- **STEP #2: Equation to find Cindy's body fat percentage:**
  - ✓ (Body Weight - Lean Body Mass) ÷ Body Weight = ANSWER, then multiply answer by 100 for a percentage.
  - ✓ **ANSWER = (143 - 106) = 37 ÷ 143 = 0.2587 x 100 = 25.87% percent body fat for this female**

WOMEN: COMPLETE MEASUREMENT & ASSESSMENT and RECORD FINAL INFORMATION HERE:

1. What's your weight? _____
2. What's your measured waist? _____
3. What's your measured hip? _____
4. What's your measured forearm? _____
5. What's your measured wrist? _____
6. What's your lean body weight? _____
7. What's your body fat percentage? _____

ASSESSMENT & MEASUREMENT #4: Pre and Post Skin Fold Caliper Device: (50 points for each measurement & assessment day; measure every 5 weeks). *NOTE: WOMEN MEASURE THE WOMEN & MEN MEASURE THE MEN.*

Taking a skinfold measurement is a standard method for determining body fat composition.

Equipment: Skin-fold caliper

Procedure: Estimation of body fat by skinfold thickness measurement (all measurements will be measured in mm = millimeters). Measure four different standard anatomical sites around the body (see below). A partner pinches and pulls the skin away from the muscle tissue (see figure below). Apply the caliper on the skin at the following sites on the body:

- middle area of the triceps
- back of the arm
- middle area of the biceps
- middle area of the shoulder blade (subscapularis)
- abdominal area/1-inch from the belly button.

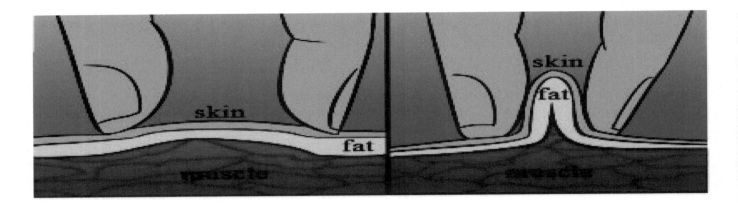

To finalize the measurements: 1.) record all measurements; 2.) add the total mm; 3.) record the final fat % using the chart on page 51.

Pre-Measurements	**Post-Measurements 1**	**Post-Measurements 2**
1. Triceps: ____mm	1. Triceps: ____ mm	1. Triceps: ____mm
2. Biceps: ____mm	2. Biceps: ____mm	2. Biceps: ____mm
3. Shoulder: ____mm	3. Shoulder: ____mm	3. Shoulder: ____mm
4. Abdominal: ____mm	4. Abdominal: ____mm	4. Abdominal: ____mm
5. Add Total mm: _____	5. Add Total mm: _____	5. Add Total mm: _____
6. Fat Percentage: _____	6. Fat Percentage: _____	6. Fat Percentage: _____

*Normal Ideal Body Fat %

The ideal body fat percentage is the most difficult question to answer. Since all people are not composed the same way, body fat percentages will vary for most individuals. Variations are due in part to genetics, sex, age, and muscular development or deterioration.

An individual may perform better at a higher or lower body fat than another person of the same age.

For men:
Up to age 30: 9% -15%
30 – 50: 11% -17%
50 and older: 12% - 19%

For women:
Up to age 30: 14% - 21%
30-50: 15% - 23%
50 and older: 16% - 25%

USE THIS CHART TO FIND THE FINAL FAT % ANSWERS. RECORD BELOW:

1. Final fat % using caliper device: _____

2. Final fat % from equations: _____

MEN				WOMEN			
Total mm	Age 16-29	Age 30-49	Age 50+	Total mm	Age 16-29	Age 30-49	Age 50+
20	8.1	12.1	12.5	14	9.4	14.1	17
22	9.2	13.2	13.9	16	11.2	15.7	18.6
24	10.2	14.2	15.1	18	12.7	17.1	20.1
26	11.2	15.2	16.3	20	14.1	18.4	21.4
28	12.1	16.1	17.4	22	15.4	19.5	22.6
30	12.9	16.9	18.5	24	16.5	20.6	23.7
35	14.7	18.7	20.8	26	17.6	21.5	24.8
40	16.3	20.3	22.8	28	18.6	22.4	25.7
45	17.7	21.8	24.7	30	19.5	23.3	26.6
50	19	23	26.3	35	21.6	25.2	28.6
55	20.2	24.2	27.8	40	23.4	26.8	30.3
60	21.2	25.3	29.1	45	25	28.3	31.9
65	22.2	26.3	30.4	50	26.5	29.6	33.2
70	23.2	27.2	31.5	55	27.8	30.8	34.6
75	24	28	32.6	60	29.1	31.9	35.7
80	24.8	28.8	33.7	65	30.2	32.9	36.7
85	25.6	29.6	34.6	70	31.2	33.9	37.7
90	26.3	30.3	35.5	75	32.2	34.7	38.6
95	27	31	36.5	80	33.1	35.6	39.5
100	27.6	31.7	37.3	85	34	36.3	40.4
110	28.8	32.9	38.8	90	34.8	37.1	41.1
120	29.9	34	40.2	95	35.6	37.8	41.9
130	31	35	41.5	100	36.3	38.5	42.6
140	31.9	36	42.8	110	37.7	39.7	43.9
150	32.8	36.8	43.9	120	39	40.8	45.1
160	33.6	37.7	45	130	40.2	41.9	46.2
170	34.4	38.5	46	140	41.3	42.9	47.3
180	35.2	39.2	47	150	42.3	43.8	48.2
190	35.9	39.9	47.9	160	43.2	44.7	49.1
200	36.5	40.6	48.8	170	44.6	45.5	50
				180	45	46.2	50.8
				190	45.8	46.9	51.6
				200	46.6	47.6	52.3

MEASUREMENT & ASSESSMENT #5A: Flexibility: (25 points for each measurement)

Equipment: A Wooden Ruler or yardstick.

Procedure: This test involves sitting on the floor with legs stretched out straight ahead. Remove the shoes. The toes of the feet are pointed towards the sky. Both knees should be locked and pressed flat to the floor. With both palms facing downward, comfortably reach forward toward the toes with both hands. Ensure that the hands remain at the same level. The student reaches out and holds the position for five seconds. Record the distance in inches away (negative inches) or past (positive inches) the big toe. No jerking movements are allowed during this five-second stretch.

WRITE GRADE FOR THIS EXERCISE

    A. PRE-MEASUREMENT 1: _____

    B. POST-MEASUREMENT 2: _____

    C. POST-MEASUREMENT 3: _____

    D. POST-MEASUREMENT 4: _____

SIT & REACH ASSESSMENT CHARTS FOR MEN & WOMEN

Grade	Men		Women	
	Cm	inches	cm	inches
Super	> +27	> +10.5	> +30	> +11.5
Excellent	+17 to +27	+6.5 to +10.5	+21 to +30	+8.0 to +11.5
Good	+6 to +16	+2.5 to +6.0	+11 to +20	+4.5 to +7.5
Average	0 to +5	0 to +2.0	+1 to +10	+0.5 to +4.0
Fair	-8 to -1	-3.0 to -0.5	-7 to 0	-2.5 to 0
Poor	-20 to -9	-7.5 to -3.5	-15 to -8	-6.0 to -3.0
Very Poor	< -20	< -7.5	< -15	< -6.0

MEASUREMENT & ASSESSMENT #5B: FINAL FLEXIBILTY ASSESSMENT

Stretch routine before or after a warm-up: (See Static and Dynamic Stretches pages 132-139)
250 points = (25 stretches @ 10 points each).

Procedure: The instructor uses various stretches throughout the term to assist with the flexibility. During the final week of the term each individual student will perform stretches, as the instructor calls out 25 stretches of choice. For all stretches correctly performed a check mark will be awarded for 10 points each. For each stretch performed incorrectly the students will receive zero points and a blank alongside each number.

1. Stretch: _____
2. Stretch: _____
3. Stretch: _____
4. Stretch: _____
5. Stretch: _____
6. Stretch: _____
7. Stretch: _____
8. Stretch: _____
9. Stretch: _____
10. Stretch: _____
11. Stretch: _____
12. Stretch: _____
13. Stretch: _____
14. Stretch: _____
15. Stretch: _____
16. Stretch: _____
17. Stretch: _____
18. Stretch: _____
19. Stretch: _____
20. Stretch: _____
21. Stretch: _____
22. Stretch: _____
23. Stretch: _____
24. Stretch: _____
25. Stretch: _____

THE BODY CORE

The center of all power and strength in the human body originates from the core of the body. Abdominal muscular strength and endurance are essential for core stability and back support. The body core consists of these muscle groups: abdominals, oblique's (side-lower rib cage), erectors of the lower back, gluteal (buttocks), upper quadriceps, upper hamstrings (gluteal thigh-in), hip flexors, and the groin area. Some example movements performed in the body core are the hip extension, hip flexion, abdominal flexion, back extension, torso rotation, lateral extension, and flexion, hip adduction, and hip abduction.

An athlete or any physically fit person is only as strong as his or her weakest link. If an individual is weak or inflexible within the core, he or she will have little chance of maximizing their potential. The core is the center that coordinates all ground-based human movements. Focusing strength-training attention on the core is of the highest importance. The more "quality" training performed with the core in the standing position and with ground-based calisthenics (movement), the more potential the athlete has to transfer the training to the athletic arena.

MEASUREMENT & ASSESSMENT #6: V-UPS/ SIT-UPS: (25 points)

The sit-up (v-ups) test measures the strength and endurance of the abdominals. Count how many sit-ups in 60 seconds, and then check and rate based on the chart below.

Procedure: Position the knees in the bent position and the soles of the feet flat on the floor. Place both hands on the largest part of the thighs. On the start command, perform the sit-up exercise for 60 seconds by continuously sliding the hands up and down the thighs. Touch the kneecaps and back down.

GRADE MEASUREMENT & ASSESSMENT FOR MEN'S SIT-UPS: (25 points each)

    A. PRE-MEASUREMENT 1: _____

    B. POST- MEASUREMENT 2: _____

    C. POST-MEASUREMENT 3: _____

    D. POST-MEASUREMENT 4: _____

MEN'S ASSESSMENT CHART FOR SIT-UPS

Grade / Age	18-25	26-35	36-45	46-55	56-65	65+
Excellent	> 49	> 45	> 41	> 35	> 31	> 28
Good	44-49	40-45	35-41	29-35	25-31	22-28
Above Average	39-43	35-39	30-34	25-28	21-24	19-21
Average	35-38	31-34	27-29	22-24	17-20	15-18
Below Average	31-34	29-30	23-26	18-21	13-16	11-14
Poor	25-30	22-28	17-22	13-17	9-12	7-10
Very Poor	< 25	< 22	< 17	< 13	< 9	< 7

GRADE MEASUREMENT & ASSESSMENT FOR WOMEN'S SIT-UPS: (25 points each)

A. PRE-MEASUREMENT 1: _____

B. POST- MEASUREMENT 2: _____

C. POST-MEASUREMENT 3: _____

D. POST-MEASUREMENT 4: _____

WOMEN'S ASSESSMENT CHART FOR SIT-UPS

Grade / Age	18-25	26-35	36-45	46-55	56-65	65+
Excellent	> 43	> 39	> 33	> 27	> 24	> 23
Good	37-43	33-39	27-33	22-27	18-24	17-23
Above Average	33-36	29-32	23-26	18-21	13-17	14-16
Average	29-32	25-28	19-22	14-17	10-12	11-13
Below Average	25-28	21-24	15-18	10-13	7-9	5-10
Poor	18-24	13-20	7-14	5-9	3-6	2-4
Very Poor	< 18	< 13	< 7	< 5	< 3	< 2

MEASUREMENT & ASSESSMENT #7: PUSH-UPS - A test to measure upper body strength and endurance: (25 points for each measurement & assessment day)

Procedure: Perform a standard "military style" pushup with the hands, and the toes are touching the floor. Position the hands on the side of the chest as the back is locked straight at a slight angle. A man or woman has the option of using the "bent knee / modified" position or the standard push up. If a man decides to perform a modified push up, he will use the women's' scale to record and grade his answers. If a woman decides to perform the "standard military push up," she will use the men's' scale to record and grade her answers.

Procedure for modified push-ups: Kneel on the floor, hands on either side of the chest and keep the back straight. If a student stops at any time during this assignment, the exercise is over. Perform as many "continuous" push-ups as possible until exhaustion. Count the total number of push-ups performed.

GRADE MEASUREMENT & ASSESSMENT FOR "STANDARD" PUSH-UPS (25 points each)

    A. PRE-MEASUREMENT 1: _____

    B. POST- MEASUREMENT 2: _____

    C. POST-MEASUREMENT 3: _____

    D. POST-MEASUREMENT 4: _____

MEN'S ASSESSMENT CHART FOR PUSH-UPS

Grade / Age	17-19	20-29	30-39	40-49	50-59	60-65
Excellent	> 56	> 47	> 41	> 34	> 31	> 30
Good	47-56	39-47	34-41	28-34	25-31	24-30
Above average	35-46	30-39	25-33	21-28	18-24	17-23
Average	19-34	17-29	13-24	11-20	9-17	6-16
Below average	11-18	10-16	8-12	6-10	5-8	3-5
Poor	4-10	4-9	2-7	1-5	1-4	1-2
Very Poor	< 4	< 4	< 2	0	0	0

GRADE MEASUREMENT & ASSESSMENT FOR "MODIFIED" PUSH-UPS: (25 points each)
CHART FOR WOMEN MODIFIED (Knees on Ground push-ups)

A. PRE-MEASUREMENT 1: _____

B. POST- MEASUREMENT 2: _____

C. POST-MEASUREMENT 3: _____

D. POST-MEASUREMENT 4: _____

WOMEN'S ASSESSMENT CHART FOR PUSH-UPS

Grade / Age	17-19	20-29	30-39	40-49	50-59	60-65
Excellent	> 35	> 36	> 37	> 31	> 25	> 23
Good	27-35	30-36	30-37	25-31	21-25	19-23
Above Average	21-27	23-29	22-30	18-24	15-20	13-18
Average	11-20	12-22	10-21	8-17	7-14	5-12
Below average	6-10	7-11	5-9	4-7	3-6	2-4
Poor	2-5	2-6	1-4	1-3	1-2	1
Very Poor	0-1	0-1	0	0	0	0

MEASUREMENT & ASSESSMENT 8: MEN'S SQUATS: (25 points)

Purpose: Lower body muscle endurance

Procedure: Stand straight with the feet at shoulder's width apart. Place the hands on the hips. Squat down gently, as the knees bend at a perfect 90-degree angle (parallel to the floor). Angles should be not seen in the legs during the exercise. Perform exercise for 60 seconds

GRADE MEASUREMENT & ASSESSMENTS FOR MEN SQUATS (25 points each)

  A. PRE-MEASUREMENT 1: _____

  B. POST- MEASUREMENT 2: _____

  C. POST-MEASUREMENT 3: _____

  D. POST-MEASUREMENT 4: _____

MEN'S ASSESSMENT CHART FOR SQUATS

Grade / Age	18-25	26-35	36-45	46-55	56-65	65+
Excellent	> 49	> 45	> 41	> 35	> 31	> 28
Good	44-49	40-45	35-41	29-35	25-31	22-28
Above average	39-43	35-39	30-34	25-38	21-24	19-21
Average	35-38	31-34	27-29	22-24	17-20	15-18
Below Average	31-34	29-30	23-26	18-21	13-16	11-14
Poor	25-30	22-28	17-22	13-17	9-12	7-10
Very Poor	< 25	< 22	< 17	< 9	< 9	< 7

GRADE MEASUREMENT & ASSESSMENT FOR WOMEN'S SQUATS (25 points each)

    A. PRE-MEASUREMENT 1: _____

    B. POST- MEASUREMENT 2: _____

    C. POST-MEASUREMENT 3: _____

    D. POST-MEASUREMENT 4: _____

WOMEN'S ASSESSMENT CHART FOR SQUATS

Grade / Age	18-25	26-35	36-45	46-55	56-65	65+
Excellent	> 43	> 39	> 33	> 27	> 24	> 23
Good	37-43	33-39	27-33	22-27	18-24	17-23
Above average	33-36	29-32	23-26	18-21	13-17	14-16
Average	29-32	25-28	19-22	14-17	10-12	11-13
Below Average	25-28	21-24	15-18	10-13	7-9	5-10
Poor	18-24	13-20	7-14	5-9	3-6	2-4
Very Poor	< 18	< 20	< 7	< 5	< 3	< 2

MEASUREMENTS AND ASSESSMENTS #9: MUSCLE ENDURANCE CIRCUIT TRAINING: (25 points)

Purpose: Overall muscle endurance and strength throughout the entire body;

Assignment: The instructor designates a time to complete a weight circuit using 10-15 stations. Each student will perform weight-bearing exercises using techniques taught by the instructor. Use a full range of motion, a moderate pace, and proper breathing techniques.

CIRCUIT EXERCISE TEST: THE GOAL: 10 REPETITIONS AT EACH MACHINE IN A DESIGNATED TIME FRAME:

CIRCLE THE TIME USED: 15 secs / 12 secs / 10secs

PRE-CIRCUIT ASSESSMENT 1:

TIME USED: _____   NO# OF REPETITIONS PERFORMED: _____

POST-CIRCUIT ASSESSMENT 2:

TIME USED: _____   NO# OF REPETITIONS PERFORMED: _____

POST-CIRCUIT ASSESSMENT 3:

TIME USED: _____   NO# OF REPETITIONS PERFORMED: _____

POST-CIRCUIT ASSESSMENT 4:

TIME USED: _____   NO# OF REPETITIONS PERFORMED: _____

HEIGHT CONVERSION CHART FOR BMI CALCULATIONS

m	inches	feet	and inches	m	inches	feet	and inches
1.36	53 1/2	4	5 1/2	1.67	66	5	6
1.37	54	4	6	1.69	66 1/2	5	6 1/2
1.38	54 1/2	4	6 1/2	1.70	67	5	7
1.40	55	4	7	1.71	67 1/2	5	7 1/2
1.41	55 1/2	4	7 1/2	1.73	68	5	8
1.42	56	4	8	1.74	68 1/2	5	8 1/2
1.43	56 1/2	4	8 1/2	1.75	69	5	9
1.45	57	4	9	1.76	69 1/2	5	9 1/2
1.46	57 1/2	4	9 1/2	1.78	70	5	10
1.47	58	4	10	1.79	70 1/2	5	10 1/2
1.48	58 1/2	4	10 1/2	1.80	71	5	11
1.50	59	4	11	1.81	71 1/2	5	11 1/2
1.51	59 1/2	4	11 1/2	1.83	72	6	0
1.52	60	5	0	1.84	72 1/2	6	1/2
1.54	60 1/2	5	1/2	1.85	73	6	1
1.55	61	5	1	1.87	73 1/2	6	1 1/2
1.56	61 1/2	5	1 1/2	1.88	74	6	2
1.57	62	5	2	1.89	74 1/2	6	2 1/2
1.59	62 1/2	5	2 1/2	1.90	75	6	3
1.60	63	5	3	1.92	75 1/2	6	3 1/2
1.61	63 1/2	5	3 1/2	1.93	76	6	4
1.62	64	5	4	1.94	76 1/2	6	4 1/2
1.64	64 1/2	5	4 1/2	1.95	77	6	5
1.65	65	5	5	1.97	77 1/2	6	5 1/2
1.66	65 1/2	5	5 1/2	1.98	78	6	6

WEIGHT CONVERSION CHART FOR BMI CALCULATIONS

Kilograms	Pounds	Kilograms	Pounds	Kilograms	Pounds	Kilograms	Pounds	Kilograms
40	88.184	70	154.323	100	220.462	130	286.6	130
41	90.389	71	156.528	101	222.666	131	288.805	131
42	92.594	72	158.732	102	224.871	132	291.01	132
43	94.798	73	160.937	103	227.076	133	293.214	133
44	97.003	74	163.142	104	229.28	134	295.419	134
45	99.208	75	165.346	105	231.485	135	297.624	135
46	101.412	76	167.551	106	233.689	136	299.828	136
47	103.617	77	169.755	107	235.894	137	302.033	137
48	105.821	78	171.96	108	238.099	138	304.237	138
49	108.026	79	174.165	109	240.303	139	306.442	139
50	110.231	80	176.369	110	242.508	140	308.647	140
51	112.435	81	178.574	111	244.713	141	310.851	141
52	114.64	82	180.779	112	246.917	142	313.056	142
53	116.844	83	182.983	113	249.122	143	315.261	143
54	119.049	84	185.188	114	251.326	144	317.465	144
55	121.254	85	187.392	115	253.531	145	319.67	145
56	123.458	86	189.597	116	255.736	146	321.874	146
57	125.663	87	191.802	117	257.94	147	324.079	147
58	127.868	88	194.006	118	260.145	148	326.284	148
59	130.072	89	196.211	119	262.35	149	328.488	149
60	132.277	90	198.416	120	264.554	150	330.693	150
61	134.481	91	200.62	121	266.759	151	332.898	151
62	136.686	92	202.825	122	268.963	152	335.102	152
63	138.891	93	205.029	123	271.168	153	337.307	153
64	141.095	94	207.234	124	273.373	154	339.511	154
65	143.3	95	209.439	125	275.577	155	341.716	155
66	145.505	96	211.643	126	277.782	156	343.921	156
67	147.709	97	213.848	127	279.987	157	346.125	157
68	149.914	98	216.053	128	282.191	158	348.33	158
69	152.118	99	218.257	129	284.396	159	350.534	159

WEEKLY FOOD LOG JOURNAL

Record the food you eat throughout the day for 2-4 weeks (see daily food log page 67). Do your best to apply learned concepts from this workbook. At the completion of each day add the total fats, calories, carbohydrates, and proteins. The goal is to create healthy choices and to feed your cells with quality foods enriched with vitamins and minerals (see page 18-21). Let's be attentive to how many pounds we can lose or gain in a healthy fun way. REMEMBER: Moderation = "occasionally in smaller amounts;"

LIMIT YOUR CANDIES, ALCOHOL, AND OTHER UNHEALTHY CRAVINGS.

Suggestions for Eating Healthy Foods

Proteins: The foods that are high in protein are: eggs (preferable egg whites or use 1 whole egg remember the yolks are high in cholesterol), fish of your choice, skinless chicken, lean red meat, nuts, soy milk, tofu, pumpkin seeds, sunflower seeds, yogurt, low fat milk, low fat cottage cheese.

Carbohydrates: Whole grains like: barley, bulgur, buckwheat, quinoa, oats, whole wheat, whole grain breads, brown rice, white rice, potatoes, whole wheat pasta or multigrain pasta, fruits, vegetables, beans, lentils, dried peas, whole grain cereals (100% bran), and oatmeal.

Salads: Romaine Lettuce has the best overall nutritional values over other lettuce varieties. Choose dressings that are vinaigrette based rather than cream based.

Drinks: Consume more water than sugary drinks, be sure to get at least eight 8 oz. glasses per day (64oz.). Other options are fruit and vegetable juices with ingredients such as: carrots, cucumber, celery, kale, spinach, romaine lettuce, concord grape juice, fresh lemon juice in water, or make your own smoothie. Moderation is the key when craving sweet drinks, don't overdo it.

Desserts – Look up your favorite low-cal dessert. You can find some of these favorites in the supermarket:

- Ciao Bella Adonia Greek Frozen Yogurt Bars in Wild Blueberry
- Newman's Own Organics Oatmeal Chocolate Chip Cookies
- So Delicious Dairy-Free Almond Milk Cherry Amaretto Frozen Dessert
- Stonyfield Oikos Chocolate Greek Frozen Yogurt
- Edy's Fruit Bars Coconut, Pineapple, Orange Variety Pack
- Skinny Cow Mint Ice Cream Sandwiches
- Jolly Llama Sorbet SqueezUps Peach Flavor
- Blue Bunny Champ Snack-Size Ice Cream Cones
- Immaculate Baking Co. Vanilla Sugar Organic Cookie Dough
- Lucy's Gluten-Free Brownie Cakes
- Amy's Organic Pound Cake
- Kozy Shack Chocolate Rice Pudding
- Weight Watchers Giant Latte Bar and Sorbet Bars
- Quaker Chewy Chocolate Chip Granola Bar
- Jell-O Pudding Cups
- South Beach Diet Snack Bar Delights
- Fage Strawberry Goji Yogurt
- Healthy Choice Moca Swirl Bar
- Healthy Choice Fudge Bar
- Orville Redenbacher Smart Pop Mini Bags
- Nilla Wafers Reduced Fat
- Nabisco 100 Calorie Snack Packs
- Skinny Cow Chocolate Fudge Brownie Ice
- Jell-O Mousse Temptations
- Yoplait Delights
- Cream Cup
- Ciao Bella Blood Orange Singles
- Baked Kettle Chips

CONVERSIONS AND MEASUREMENTS FOR CALORIE COUNTING

- Fat: 1 gram = 9 Calories
- Protein: 1 gram = 4 Calories
- Carbohydrates: 1 gram = 4 Calories
- Alcohol: 1 gram = 7 Calories

Volume
- 1 gallon (3.786 liters; 3,786 ml) = 4 quarts
- 1 quart (0.946 liter; 946 ml) = 4 cups or 2 pints
- 1 cup (237 ml) 8 fluid ounces = ½ pint = 16 tablespoons
- 2 tablespoons (30 ml) = 1 fluid ounce
- 1 tablespoon *(15* ml) = 3 teaspoons
- 1 pint = 2 cups

Weight
- 1 pound (16 ounces) = 453.6 grams
- 1 ounce = 28.35 grams
- 3½ ounces = 100 grams

How to measure portions at restaurants
You have a measuring cup right there in the palm of your hand. A spoon is on your finger! Here are some ways you can use your hands to measure portions.

- Fist = 1 cup of fruit or 1 medium whole, raw fruit
- Thumb = 1 ounce of cheese or meat
- Fingertip = Approximately 1 teaspoon
- Tip of Thumb = Approximately 1 tablespoon
- One Cupped Hand = 1 or 2 ounces of dry goods (nuts, cereal, pretzels)

DAILY FOOD LOG-IN CHART

FOOD LOG	Monday	Tuesday	Wednesday	Thursday	Friday	Saturday	Sunday
Breakfast							
Snack							
Lunch							
Snack							
Dinner							
Snack							

COACHES' CORNER

This section is dedicated to male and female coaches at all levels who coach and train amateur and professional athletes. Since coaches have limited time throughout the day, the charts in this workbook on the F.I.T.T. principle (page 38-39) and circuit training routines (pages 78-79) can assist all coaches and individuals who have busy schedules. In the nutrition section of this workbook, the coaches and their staffs can use equations and gain ideas for good eating habits. Our society has become so fast-paced that many people are replacing healthy meals with fast foods. We do not realize that our fast food choices lack the essential vitamins the body needs to function properly. As our bodies age, we begin to lose certain physiological functions. However, by maintaining good eating habits and taking our essential vitamins, we can delay the loss of the body's functions. Bone loss, memory, and eyesight are some physiological functions that can deteriorate during the ageing process. However, all these functions can be stabilized and made stronger by taking in the necessary vitamins our body needs.

Restaurant and fast food choices can be made simple by choosing the proper foods and having the discipline for portion control. This coaches' corner section is a reminder for all of us to focus our attention towards fitness for life. We must concentrate on STAYING in good physical health for the rest of our lives.

Through focused efforts on our health, we can spend more time with family, keep our body in good physical condition, and have more energy to coach our students. As coaches, we need to lead by example by our physical appearance. On game days, during warm-ups or the game, all eyes are on the staff. One of the most interesting topics in coaching today is the mood or mindset of our coaches. Our character is most evident during the practice week, at games, after games, and during meetings. When we are overwhelmed, exercise helps alleviate stress and tension as exercise stimulates positive moods and thoughts. Coaches can start a solid fitness routine with their student by scheduling 60-90 minute workout sessions in the morning. Getting into the habit of working out at a set time will help you to be more successful towards your goals. The key is to have a series of different time slots for various workout routines in the event of normal interruptions. Below are 12 life-altering positive benefits when we exercise.

- Reduction in anxiety and stress
- Positive mood enhancement
- Reduced tension
- Lower blood pressure
- Control blood sugar levels (diabetes)
- Enhanced digestion and excretory functions
- Strengthens bones (limiting osteoporosis)
- Controls weight
- Prevents cancer
- Keeps the lungs strong
- Keeps the heart strong
- Keeps blood vessels clear

Exercise with a Partner

Exercising with a partner or trainer is the key to staying motivated and accountable with your exercise goals. A study by Dr. Pamela Rackow from the Institute of Applied Health Sciences at the University of Aberdeen found that individuals are known to exercise more frequently when emotional support is involved in an exercise routine. By using emotional and instrumental groups, the study concluded that people exercised more when an exercise partner offered emotional support and encouragement, rather than practical support.

Quick Workout Charts for Busy Schedules

Several workout charts are located in the appendix and are designed to create a fast, safe, calorie burning fitness routine. By keeping the heart rate in a calorie burning zone (see page 40), we can cut weight quickly and efficiently. More importantly, these charts will help you fit a variety of workouts into your schedule without becoming bored and stagnate. The quick fitness routine charts are:

- F.I.T.T. principle exercise charts (page 38-39)
- Weekly cardiovascular fitness chart (page 117-118)
- For the best results in exercise and fitness our daily meal plan must healthy (food log page 67)
- Static and dynamic stretches for flexibility (page 132--139)
- Rubric charts for assessing your progress every 2-3 months (page 129-131)

Even though a 3-4 day per week exercise routine with a good meal plan is a great start, using a 5-6 day per week exercise routine gives better results. Lastly, review, read, and incorporate the simple 5 components of physical fitness (see page 8).

Final Thoughts

Leftovers

Try not to use one large container to store leftovers such as casseroles, side dishes, or pasta. Instead, separate them into individually-sized containers. Thus, when we reach into the refrigerator to find something to eat, we retrieve smaller helpings. Breaking the serving size into single servings will help limit food intake with no additional effort.

Have a Big Salad

When we eat salads before lunch or dinner, it is a sure-fire way to keep from overeating. Salads will help curb the appetite and give a sense of fullness. The best lettuce choice is romaine or preferably red leaf. These two selections are by far more nutritious than iceberg lettuce. Also, don't forget to load up your salad with other vegetables. You may also include lean meats and fruits. Your choice of salad dressings should be reduced in calories, vinaigrettes, Italian, tomato based, or honey based. Remember creamy white dressings have more mayonnaise, which in most cases have more fats and calories.

Treat Yourself in Moderation

When you make healthier meal choices, you allow yourself to have a treat meal without the guilt. This helps eliminate the feeling of deprivation and helps maintain focus. Don't forget that deprivation can cause overeating. Learn how to eat a variety of good nutritional foods throughout the week, while still being able to have cheat meals. Consistency with a balanced caloric intake along with exercise is the key to a better life. If you understand and concentrate on these healthy tasks, you will not need to use the word "diet" again. You will be able to say, "I EAT CLEAN" or "I EAT HEALTHY."

Finally, we must understand that we have good days and bad days. Eating three snicker bars, a half-gallon of ice cream, and two-family size bags of Ruffles will add a tremendous amount of guilt. However, we cannot beat ourselves up and let the "guilt" overwhelm us. Instead, let's become focused on the next several days after the mega calorie cheat day. It is imperative that the cheat day does not continue day after day. Look forward to healthy choices each day, get back into the saddle and focus on a healthy food plan.

The data collected in this Kinesiology workbook should be used as a guide, but not as a primary source of reference. Before starting any physical fitness program, one should always consult with their medical physician.

REFERENCES

1. Hales, Dianne; Wadesworth Cengage Learning, 2010. *An Invitation to Health.*

2. Retrieved from https://www.fda.gov/Food/GuidanceRegulation/RetailFoodProtection/FoodCode/ucm 2018345.htm.

3. The United States Department of Health and Human Services. Healthy People 2010: 2nd Edition. Washington, DC; November 2000. *Understanding and Improving Health.*

4. Liebman, Bonnie; Fitness News #2; Health Letter, pages 2-7, December 2008. *Nutrition In Action.*

5. Top End Sports Network. 1997-2010. Retrieved from http://www.topendsports.com.

6. Wells, K.F. & Dillon, E.K. Research Quarterly, 23.115-118, 1952. *The sit and reach: A test of back and leg flexibility.*

7. 2000 CDC growth charts. Data from NHES II (1963 to 1965) and III (1966 to 1970), and NHANES I (1971 to 1974), II (1976 to 1980), and III (1988 to 1994). *BMI growth charts specifically excluded NHANES III data for children older than 6 years.*

8. Tenth Edition of the RDAs (1989) and Scientific Evaluation of Dietary Reference Intakes (1997, 1998, and 2000). *Recommended Daily Dietary Intakes.*

9. Donatelle, Rebecca. Eighth edition; Pearson, Benjamin Cummings, 2009. *Health the Basics.*

10. U.S. Department of Agriculture and Department of Health and Human Services (2000).

11. Mourao DM; Bressan J, Campbell WW, Mattes RD; Department of Foods and Nutrition, Purdue University. International Journal of Obesity. 2007 Nov (11):1688-95. *Effects of food form on appetite and energy intake in lean and obese young adults.*

12. The Glycemic Index Calculator. Retrieved from www.glycemicindexcalculator.com/.

13. Glycemic Index and Glycemic Load Charts. Retrieved from http://www.shaklee.com/pws/library/products/wm_gi_gl_tables.pdf.

14. AMERICAN COUNCIL ON EXERCISE. Retrieved from www.acefitness.org.

15. Dr. Michael Olpin; Weber State University. *Benefits of Aerobic Conditioning & Cardiovascular Benefits.* Retrieved from www.weber.edu/molpin/exercisebenefits.html.

16. Philip Moeller; U.S. News & World Report LP, Aug 16, 2012. *A Predictor of Longer Life.*

17. Delish Food Recipes. Retrieved from http://www.delish.com.

18. Diabetes Spectrum 2011 May; 24 (2): 100 -106. Retrieved from https://doi.org/10.2337/diaspect.24.2.100.

19. Retrieved from https://www.myfooddiary.com/resources/ask_the_expert/aerobic_vs_anaerobic.asp.

20. American Journal of Nutrition. Retrieved from https://academic.oup.com/ajcn/article/76/1/281S/4824165.

21. Janette C Brand-Miller, Susanna HA Holt, Dorota B Pawlak, Joanna McMillan. The American Journal of Clinical Nutrition, Volume 76, Issue 1, 1 July 2002. *Glycemic Index and Obesity*

22. The American Diabetes Association. Diabetes Care 2014 Jan; 37(Supplement 1): S14-S80. https://doi.org/10.2337/dc14-S014. *Standards of Medical Care in Diabetes.*

23. Retrieved from http://www.stretching-exercises-guide.com/foam-roller-exercises.html#

24. GZ MacDonald, MDH Penney, ME Mullaley, AL Cuconato, CDJ Drake, DG Behm, DC Button. Journal of Strength & Conditioning Research. March 2013 Volume 27,3 p 812-821. *An Acute Bout of Self Myofascial Release Increases Range of Motion without a Subsequent Decrease in Muscle Activation or Force.*

25. KC Healey, DL Hatfield, P Blanpied, LR Dorfman, D Riebe. The Journal of Strength & Conditioning Research; Post acceptance April 2013. *The Effects of Self Myofascial Release with Foam Rolling on Performance.*

26. T Okamoto, M Masuhara, K Ikuta. Journal of Strength & Conditioning Research, 9 April 2013. *Acute Effects of Self Myofascial Release Using a Foam Roller on Arterial Function.*

27. Retrieved from https://en.wikipedia.org/wiki/Kinesiology

28. Richard Weil, MEd, CDE, June 2017. *Health Facts.*

29. Retrieved from https://www.onhealth.com/content/1/muscle_soreness /

30. Retrieved from https://www.livestrong.com/article/331420-why-is-muscle-endurance-important/

31. Retrieved from https://www.humankinetics.com/excerpts/excerpts/physical-activity-the-focus-of-kinesiology

32. Marcia Nelms, Kathryn P. Sucher. *Nutrition Therapy and Pathophysiology. 2nd edition.*

33. Retrieved from https://www.aafp.org/home.html;

34. Heyward, Vivian H.; Gibson, Ann, April 23, 2014, Human Kinetics. *Advanced Fitness Assessment and Exercise Prescription. 7th Edition.*

35. Retrieved from https://www.calculator.net/bmr-calculator.html

36. Retrieved from https://www.cdc.gov/nchs/fastats/exercise.htm

37. Retrieved from https://www.nhs.uk/Livewell/fitness/Pages/why-do-I-feel-pain-after-exercise.aspx

38. Warpeha, Joseph. NSCA's Performance Training Journal 2004. *Upper Body Plyometrics.*

39. Renfro, Gregory Strength and Conditioning Journal June 1999. *Summer Plyometric Training for Football and its Effect of Speed and Agility.*

40. Barnes, Michael. *NSCA: Agility for Football.*

41. Woody, Kyle. Stack Mag May 2009. *Linear Speed Training for Football.*

42. Retrieved from https://www.livestrong.com/article/139540 the best football workouts/#ixzz1xoTRmhbj.

43. Duke Health. July 21, 2016. *Physical declines begin earlier than expected among U.S. adults.* Retrieved from https://www.sciencedaily.com/releases/2016/10/161004081548.htm.

44. Sagon, by Candy, August 25, 2016. Retrieved from https://www.aarp.org/health/healthy-living/info-2016/fitness-aging-physical-decline-cs.html.

45. Retrieved from https://www.cedarcoveassistedliving.com/mental-benefits-of-exercise-for-the-elderly.

APPENDIX

STRENGTH and CONDITIONING PHILOSOPHY

Although there are some differences in various methods of strength and conditioning, there are 3 common observations.

- Extremely Intense
- Organization
- Short in Duration

IMPORTANT PHYSICAL FITNESS REMINDERS

- Proper technique is essential for every exercise.
- Proper placement of all weights is essential. All weights have a rack for placement.
- Always keep weights off the floor.
- Proper attire is required.
- A spotter is mandatory when conducting heavy free bar exercises.
- Do not move weight equipment from its designated area. Return weights and weight belts to proper location.
- No food or beverage is allowed in the weight room. Place drink outside of weight room.
- Follow your program

Strength & Conditioning Objectives

The objective of a strength and conditioning program is to ensure overall physical fitness, and to provide a sound post-season, pre-season, and in-season program. A strength and conditioning program should include muscle strength, muscle endurance, cardiovascular conditioning, flexibility, and nutrition. Using free weights helps create balance and coordination, assist stabilizers (muscle that work to restrict the movement of certain joints), and synergistic muscles (the helper muscles ex: joint movement). It becomes very important to balance and stabilize your body in order for the prime mover muscles to perform.

Training with Bodyweight Movements and Lifts from the Ground

In most competitive sports, we use our feet on the ground to initiate speed, power, and good balance. This comes from using various angles of force that is apply to the ground. Once the movement has started, we use bones, joints, tendons, ligaments, stabilizer muscles, prime mover muscles, and synergistic muscles. The philosophy is to develop more athletic abilities for each athlete. If we train athletes on their feet with ground movements, their mind and body will absorb these training methods, thus preparing them for competition. We can maximize athletic potential by using ground-based lifts and activities such as the dead lift, front squat, hang clean, power clean, lunge, standing press, push-ups, push press cone drills, bag drills, ladder drills, sled drives, sled pulls and stadium stairs.

Upper Body Strength Training

Nearly every sport involves using the upper body. Pushing, pulling, grabbing involves muscle groups by using exercises that involve more than one joint at a time. You can use barbell shrugs, upright rows, and manual resistance flexion, extension, and lateral flexion to address upper body strength. Other major muscle groups to focus on include your chest, shoulders and back.

Lower Body Strength Training

A strong lower body is a must in competitive sports. Movements that affect more than one joint, such as the back squat, front squat and various single-leg maneuvers should be emphasized in all competitive weight training programs. It is important to focus on building strength in the posterior area of the body. The posterior area of the lower body is very important and can't be overlooked in competitive sports. Posterior muscles assist several muscles in the anterior portion of lower body. If the posterior muscles are weak, the stronger larger anterior muscle can over power the posterior muscles, thus causing possible pulls, strains, and even tears. The posterior muscles are encompassed by your hamstrings, glutes, and lower back. By using exercises such as the dead lift, power clean, and hip strengthening exercises such as hip flexion, extension, abduction, and adduction you will ensure there are no weaknesses in your lower body.

Using a Pyramid System for Workouts

You will notice in charts in the appendix the "pyramid" training method of strength and conditioning. Pyramid weight training starts with lighter weight matched with high repetitions. After the body is warmed up, the subsequent sets will increase in weight and decrease in repetitions. One can also do the reverse. After one or two warm up sets, start with heavy weights and low repetitions, and progress in the opposite direction by decreasing the weight and increasing the repetitions. Reverse pyramid sets are not recommended, and one should be cautious when introducing heavy weights too soon within a workout. Improper warm-ups during heavy workouts can create tendonitis and various injuries.

The Benefits of Pyramid Training

By starting light, we give our muscles, joints, and connective tissues a chance to warm up. By gradually increasing the weight, you can effectively overload the muscles, exhausting the muscle fibers to create an intense and effective routine. Remember most workouts may not give enormous results after 3-months, but after 6 to 12-months you may see strength gains, since your muscles adapt extremely well to the type of training you consistently performed.

The Body's Core

The center of all power and strength originates in the core of the body. Imagine the human body broken down into three links of a chain: the upper body (ribcage up), lower body (mid-thigh down) and core body (front, back, the sides, and midsection). The exercises performed in the core are: back extension, hip extension, hip flexion, abdominal flexion, torso rotation, lateral extension, and flexion, hip adduction, and hip abduction. If the athlete is weak or not flexible in the core, they will have little chance of maximizing their athletic potential creating limitations with the possibility of injury. The body's core is the center that regulates and assists in ground-based human movements. Focusing strength-training along with body's core is very important. The body's core consists of these muscle groups: abdominals, obliques, erectors of lower back, gluteal, upper quadriceps, upper hamstrings, hip flexors, and groin area. Body core training in the standing position along with ground-based movements creates more potential for the athlete to transfer the training to competition.

Conditioning Charts

Since a certain amount of overload is needed to increase body's physical capabilities, the body must adapt to stress during strength and conditioning training. Exercises such as plyometrics use the stretch-shortening cycle of muscles to elicit forceful contractions, resulting in an increase in power output. You should keep the volume of repetitions low and concentrate on both the upper and lower body. Some examples of plyometric exercises are medicine ball throws, heavy rope swings for the upper body, box jumps, broad jumps, bounding exercises for the lower body, and any other plyometric exercises needed within your training program.

Agility Training

In sports majority of plays involve change-of-direction, starting and stopping quickly and efficiently. Agility drills should be designed from your sport to reinforce this notion. There are two basic types of agility drills called open and closed. Open agility drills react to a stimulus. Closed agility drills have a set pattern.

Speed Training

Speed and quickness win sports competitions, so it is crucial that every aspect of your workouts focuses on how to get faster. To improve your speed, increase your stride length, stride frequency or both.

Athletic Lifts Not Isolation Lifts

What are athletic lifts? Athletic lifts are lifts that incorporate the human body's joints, muscles, tendons, and ligaments together in one lift in an explosive fashion. Athletes are better prepared to use their whole body in sports, when they train with lifts, drills and calisthenics that incorporate many muscles, tendons, ligaments, joints, and bones in a natural progression. It is important that athletes perform athletic lifts as their main emphasis when strength training. The lift is athletic when:

- More muscles, tendons, ligaments, and joints used through a wide range of motion.
- Resistance held in the hands while in a standing position.
- Increased resistance during the lift
- Faster resistance for that prescribed intensity.
- The faster the body moves around or under the resistance during the lift.

One can get strong using almost any type of strength training. However, it is best to have athletes perform athletic lifts and bodyweight calisthenics. When using weight machines, you are using one plane one dimension of movement. Thus, there is isolation of one joint or one group of muscles without having to balance or stabilize another body part. Machine lifts can be very advantageous when used at the end of a workout or during in-season training.

V. Train Athleticism

The positive qualities of the superior athlete are:
- Agility, flexibility, coordination, mental toughness, kinesthetic awareness, rapid reorientation from disorientation, strength, rapid gathering from poor positions, power, goal-driven, sport specific condition, speed, skill expertise.

- Maximize the athletic potential of the athletes in these areas and he / she will experience success.

Training Attitude

- Hard intense workouts with good solid technique on every lift.
- Always focused on becoming better every day.
- Demand within yourself focus, intensity, mental toughness, and most of all discipline.
- At each workout give a 100% effort to maximize athletic potential.

POST SEASON, PRE-SEASON, IN-SEASON CHARTS

The following charts can be used for any female or male sport, competition, non-competition, or simply getting into great physical condition. This information will assist all individuals by simply plugging-in the specific workouts for your sport. These charts will work best by applying the F.I.T.T. principle (see pages 36-39) to your specific goals.

Rest Season / Out of Season: (2-4 weeks after a season of competition): One of the most criticized areas of a strength and conditioning program is the rest season area. All athletes need mental and physical rest. During this time, the body and mind is allowed to recuperate. This restoration period will create an effort of 100% once the season starts. Many professional strength and conditioning coaches believe that a rest period brings about bad habits and most of all regression of muscle strength. Studies do show that the female and male athlete can quickly regress, especially when too much rest is applied after the competition period. Therefore, a good post-season and in-season strength and conditioning program is extremely important and should be well organized, since it is the most crucial time for an athlete to focus on gaining, maintaining, and preparing the body for the next season.

Post Season (4-6 weeks): Introduction to Strength and Conditioning Program – The beginning 4-6 weeks workout plan that has high repetitions and light weight lifting (ex: 3 days/week-45-60 min workouts).

Pre-Season (5–8 months program that concentrates on strength, power, body conditioning, and flexibility): Strength and Conditioning Program - It's a non-competition phase: ex: 3–4 days a week - 60-75 min workouts + conditioning = total 90 minutes. Remember: Once a fitness routine time goes over 90 minutes the 100% effort of the human body will start to decline significantly. This in turn can cause various injuries. After a 90 minutes workout, it is suggested to create a solid cool down stretch at 15-20 minutes.

In Season: Strength and Conditioning Program / Body Maintenance (circuit training, muscle endurance training; 3 – 4 weeks with a 30 min workout; prior to the first competition). Weekly games are called the in-season competition phase = 2 days per week with a 30 min workout. During this phase, the body is extremely tired from intense practices, mental learning, academics, employment, family time, and most of all post game exhaustion. During this phase it is normal for individuals to lose strength, but it's preferred that the decrease in strength is gradual or stay the same. One of the best programs during the time is circuit training. Circuit training creates a quick solid weight training program, and allows for a quick change over from weight training to practice. It allows the individual to use machine weights and train the body's core all in a short span of time.

ATHLETIC CHARTS

CIRCUIT TRAINING: NOVICE / BEGINNER ATHLETE

Monday: Upper Body

	Exercise	Muscle
Station 1	Flat Bench 1	Chest
Station 2	Incline Bench Press	Chest
Station 3	Chest Fly's	Chest
Station 4	Triceps Pushdowns	Triceps
Station 5	Military Press	Shoulders
Station 6	Side Lateral Raises	Shoulders
Station 7	Close Push Ups	Triceps
Station 8	Rear Pulleys	Back
Station 9	Seated Rows	Back
Station 10	Rear Raises	Shoulders
Station 11	Bicep Curls	Biceps
Station 12	Abdominal Crunches	Stomach
Station 13	Abdominal Twist	Stomach
Station 14	Shrugs	Shoulders

Tuesday: Lower Body

	Exercise	Muscle
Station 1	Stiff Leg Deadlift	Legs
Station 2	Leg Extensions	Legs
Station 3	Hamstring Curls	Legs
Station 4	Squats	Legs
Station 5	Front Lunges	Legs
Station 6	Calf Raises	Legs
Station 7	Abdominal Crunch	Stomach
Station 8	Bicycles	Stomach
Station 9	Leg Raises	Stomach
Station 10	Bent Leg Raises	Stomach
Station 11	Roman Chair	Low Back
Station 12	Front Planks	Core
Station 13	Left Side Planks	Core
Station 14	Right Side Planks	Core

Wednesday: Upper Body

	Exercise	Muscle
Station 1	Flat Bench 1	Chest
Station 2	Incline Bench Press	Chest
Station 3	Chest Fly's	Chest
Station 4	Triceps Pushdowns	Triceps
Station 5	Military Press	Shoulders
Station 6	Side Lateral Raises	Shoulders
Station 7	Close Push Ups	Triceps
Station 8	Rear Pulleys	Back
Station 9	Seated Rows	Back
Station 10	Rear Raises	Shoulders
Station 11	Bicep Curls	Biceps
Station 12	Abdominal Crunches	Stomach
Station 13	Abdominal Twist	Stomach
Station 14	Shrugs	Shoulders

Thursday: Lower Body & Maintenance

	Exercise	Muscle
Station 1	Stiff Leg Deadlift	Legs
Station 2	Leg Extensions	Legs
Station 3	Hamstring Curls	Legs
Station 4	Squats	Legs
Station 5	Front Lunges	Legs
Station 6	Calf Raises	Legs
Station 7	Abdominal Crunch	Stomach
Station 8	Bicycles	Stomach
Station 9	Leg Raises	Stomach
Station 10	Bent Leg Raises	Stomach
Station 11	Roman Chair	Low Back
Station 12	Front Planks	Core
Station 13	Left Side Planks	Core
Station 14	Right Side Planks	Core

CIRCUIT TRAINING: ADVANCED STRENGTH TRAINING ALL LEVELS

Monday: Upper Body

	Exercise	Muscle
Station 1	Upright Rows	Shoulders
Station 2	Bicep Curls	Biceps
Station 3	Triceps Extensions	Triceps
Station 4	Side Lateral Raise	Shoulders
Station 5	Triceps Push Downs	Triceps
Station 6	Jump Rope	Multi Groups
Station 7	Military Press	Shoulders
Station 8	Abdominal Crunches	Stomach
Station 9	Abdominal Twist	Stomach
Station 10	Chest Fly's	Chest
Station 11	Flat Bench 1	Chest
Station 12	Flat Bench 2	Chest
Station 13	Flat Bench 3	Chest
Station 14	Flat Bench 4	Chest
Station 15	Incline Bench Press	Chest

Tuesday: Lower Body

	Exercise	Muscle
Station 1	Stiff Leg Deadlift	Legs
Station 2	Bent Over Dumbbell Pulley	Back
Station 3	Vertical Jump	Legs
Station 4	Lat Pulley's	Back
Station 5	Seated Rows	Back
Station 6	Jump Rope	Multi Groups
Station 7	Abdominal Crunches	Stomach
Station 8	Abdominal Twist	Stomach
Station 9	Leg Extensions	Legs
Station 10	4-Way Neck	Neck
Station 11	Shrugs	Traps / Shoulders
Station 12	Squat 1	Legs
Station 13	Squat 2	Legs
Station 14	Squat 3	Legs
Station 15	Snatch	Legs

Wednesday: Upper Body

	Exercise	Muscle
Station 1	Upright Rows	Shoulders
Station 2	Bicep Curls	Biceps
Station 3	Triceps Extensions	Triceps
Station 4	Side Lateral Raise	Shoulders
Station 5	Triceps Push Downs	Triceps
Station 6	Jump Rope	Multi Groups
Station 7	Military Press	Shoulders
Station 8	Abdominal Crunches	Stomach
Station 9	Abdominal Twist	Stomach
Station 10	Chest Fly's	Chest
Station 11	Flat Bench 1	Chest
Station 12	Flat Bench 2	Chest
Station 13	Flat Bench 3	Chest
Station 14	Flat Bench 4	Chest
Station 15	Incline Bench Press	Chest

Thursday: Lower Body & Maintenance

	Exercise	Muscle
Station 1	Stiff Leg Deadlift	Legs
Station 2	Bent Over Dumbbell Pulley	Back
Station 3	Vertical Jump	Legs
Station 4	Lat Pulley	Back
Station 5	Seated Rows	Back
Station 6	Jump Rope	Multi Groups
Station 7	Abdominal Crunches	Stomach
Station 8	Abdominal Twist	Stomach
Station 9	Leg Extensions	Legs
Station 10	4-Way Neck	Neck
Station 11	Shrugs	Traps / Shoulders
Station 12	Hang Cleans	Multi Groups
Station 13	Hang Cleans	Multi Groups
Station 14	Hang Cleans	Multi Groups
Station 15	Snatch	Legs

ADVANCED STRENGTH CHARTS FOR
ATHLETIC / COMPETITION SPORTS: STRENGTH PROGRAM

POST SEASON LIFTING (1st 4 weeks after a 1 to 2-month rest after a season of competition)

EXAMPLE: POST-SEASON STRENGTH & CONDITIONING: WEEKS 1 - 4								
DAY 1	**WEEK 1**		**WEEK 2**		**WEEK 3**		**WEEK 4**	
Bench Press	Weight	Reps	Weight	Reps	Weight	Reps	Weight	Reps
	Warm-up		Warm-up		Warm-up		Warm-up	
	55%	12	58%	10	60%	10	62%	10
	60%	12	63%	10	65%	8	68%	8
	63%	12	70%	8	73%	8	75%	5
	58-61%	12	73%	8	78%	6	79%	5
			65%	10	69%	10	81%	5
							65%	10
Hang Clean	Weight	Reps	Weight	Reps	Weight	Reps	Weight	Reps
	50-54%	6	51-55%	5	53-58%	4	61%	4
	55-59%	6	56-61%	5	63-69%	4	72%	4
	61-64%	6	63-68%	5	70-73%	4	76%	4
	65-69%	6	69-72%	5	71-74%	4	80%	4
Barbell Upright Rows *(Superset with Military Push Press)*	Weight	Reps	Weight	Reps	Weight	Reps	Weight	Reps
		10		10		10		10
		10		10		10		10
		10		10		10		10
Military Push Press *(Superset with Barbell Upright Rows)*	Weight	Reps	Weight	Reps	Weight	Reps	Weight	Reps
		10		10		10		10
		10		10		10		10
		10		10		10		10
Dumbbell Curls *(Superset with Barbell Triceps Extension)*	Weight	Reps	Weight	Reps	Weight	Reps	Weight	Reps
		10		10		10		10
		10		10		10		10
		10		10		10		10
Barbell Triceps Extension *(Superset with Dumbbell Curls)*	Weight	Reps	Weight	Reps	Weight	Reps	Weight	Reps
		10		10		10		10
		10		10		10		10
		10		10		10		10
Diamond Pushups *(Superset with Weighted Torso Twist)*	Weight	Reps	Weight	Reps	Weight	Reps	Weight	Reps
		10		10		10		10
		10		10		10		10
		10		10		10		10
Weighted Torso Twist *(Superset with Diamond Pushups)*	Weight	Reps	Weight	Reps	Weight	Reps	Weight	Reps
		3x25		3x25		3x25		3x25

EXAMPLE: POST-SEASON STRENGTH & CONDITIONING: WEEKS 1 - 4								
DAY 2	**WEEK 1**		**WEEK 2**		**WEEK 3**		**WEEK 4**	
Squats	Weight	Reps	Weight	Reps	Weight	Reps	Weight	Reps
	Warm-up		Warm-up		Warm-up		Warm-up	
	61%	10	63%	10	65%	10	67%	10
	64-67%	10	66-69%	10	68-72%	8	74%	8
	70-73%	10	70-73%	8	71-74%	8	79%	6
	67-70%	10	74-80%	6	75-83%	6	85%	6
	65%	10	68%	10	70%	10	72%	8
	63%	10	64%	10	68%	10	69%	10
Power Clean	Weight	Reps	Weight	Reps	Weight	Reps	Weight	Reps
	50-54%	6	51-55%	5	53-58%	4	61%	4
	55-59%	6	56-61%	5	63-69%	4	72%	4
	61-64%	6	63-68%	5	70-73%	4	76%	4
	65-69%	6	69-72%	5	71-74%	4	80%	4
Dumbbell Deadlift *(Superset with Straight Deadlift)*	Weight	Reps	Weight	Reps	Weight	Reps	Weight	Reps
		10		10		8		6
		10		10		8		6
		10		10		8		6
Straight Deadlift *(Superset with Dumbbell Deadlift)*	Weight	Reps	Weight	Reps	Weight	Reps	Weight	Reps
		8		8		8		8
		8		8		8		8
		8		8		8		8
Lunges	Weight	Reps	Weight	Reps	Weight	Reps	Weight	Reps
		3 x 8		3 x 8		3 x 8		3 x 8
Lat Pulls to Front *(Superset with Hyper Extensions or Hamstring Curls)*	Weight	Reps	Weight	Reps	Weight	Reps	Weight	Reps
		10		10		10		10
		10		10		10		10
		10		10		10		10
Hyper Extensions or Hamstring Curls *(Superset with Lat Pulls to Front*	Weight	Reps	Weight	Reps	Weight	Reps	Weight	Reps
		10		10		10		10
		10		10		10		10
		10		10		10		10
Crunches	Weight	Reps	Weight	Reps	Weight	Reps	Weight	Reps
		4 x 35		4 x 35		4 x 40		4 x 40

EXAMPLE: POST-SEASON STRENGTH & CONDITIONING: WEEKS 1-4								
Day 3	**WEEK 1**		**WEEK 2**		**WEEK 3**		**WEEK 4**	
Incline Bench Press	**Weight**	**Reps**	**Weight**	**Reps**	**Weight**	**Reps**	**Weight**	**Reps**
	Warm-up		Warm-up		Warm-up		Warm-up	
	58%	10	60%	10	65%	10	67%	10
	63%	10	66%	10	70%	8	72%	8
	65%	8	69%	8	73%	8	75%	5
	70%	8	73%	8	76%	5	79%	5
	74%	8	77%	5	80%	5	83%	5
	60%	10	64%	10	70%	10	71%	10
Heavy Barbell Shrug	**Weight**	**Reps**	**Weight**	**Reps**	**Weight**	**Reps**	**Weight**	**Reps**
		10		10		10		10
		10		10		10		10
		10		10		10		10
Dumbbell Incline Bench Press	**Weight**	**Reps**	**Weight**	**Reps**	**Weight**	**Reps**	**Weight**	**Reps**
		10		10		10		10
		10		10		10		10
		10		10		10		10
Barbell Bent Over Rows	**Weight**	**Reps**	**Weight**	**Reps**	**Weight**	**Reps**	**Weight**	**Reps**
		10		10		10		10
		10		10		10		10
		10		10		10		10
Hanging Leg Raises or Leg Lifts *(Superset with Crunches)*	**Weight**	**Reps**	**Weight**	**Reps**	**Weight**	**Reps**	**Weight**	**Reps**
		10		10		10		10
		10		10		10		10
		10		10		10		10
Crunches *(Superset with Hanging Leg Raises or Leg Lifts)*	**Weight**	**Reps**	**Weight**	**Reps**	**Weight**	**Reps**	**Weight**	**Reps**
		4 x 35		4 x 35		4 x 40		4 x 40

EXAMPLE: PRE-SEASON STRENGTH & CONDITIONING: WEEKS 5 - 8

DAY 1	WEEK 5		WEEK 6		WEEK 7		1 Rep Max	Week
							WEEK 8	
	Weight	Reps	Weight	Reps	Weight	Reps	Weight	Reps
1. Overhead Squats		10		10		10		10
2. Lateral Lunges		6		6		6		6
3. Back Squats	Warm up	12	Warm up	12	Warm up	12	Warm up	12
	57%	8	60%	8	64%	8	64%	8
	60%	5	65%	5	70%	5	73%	4
	63%	5	68%	5	73%	5	75%	3
	65%	5	70%	5	75%	4	77%	3
2 min rest	68%	5	73%	4	78%	3	80%	3
Hang Cleans	Weight	Reps	Weight	Reps	Weight	Reps	Weight	Reps
	57%	5	60%	5	64%	5	64%	5
Explode from hips & legs	60%	5	65%	5	70%	4	73%	3
	63%	5	68%	5	73%	4	75%	3
	65%	5	70%	4	75%	3	77%	3
	68%	5	73%	4	78%	3	80%	3
Dumbbell Lunges *(Superset with Dumbbell Heavy Shrugs)*	Weight	Reps	Weight	Reps	Weight	Reps	Weight	Reps
		8		8		8		8
		8		8		8		8
		8		8		8		8
Romanian Deadlift *(small bend in knees)*	Weight	Reps	Weight	Reps	Weight	Reps	Weight	Reps
		10		10		10		10
		10		10		10		10
		10		10		10		10
Bench Press	Weight	Reps	Weight	Reps	Weight	Reps	Weight	Reps
	59%	8	63%	8	65%	8	68%	8
	64%	8	65%	6	68%	5	73%	5
	67%	6	70%	5	73%	5	76%	4
	70%	4	75%	5	76%	4	80%	3
Alt. DB Press	Weight	Reps	Weight	Reps	Weight	Reps	Weight	Reps
		5		5		5		5
		5		5		5		5
		5		5		5		5
Hammer Curls	Weight	Reps	Weight	Reps	Weight	Reps	Weight	Reps
		10		10		10		10
		10		10		10		10
		10		10		10		10
Neck Machine	Weight	Reps	Weight	Reps	Weight	Reps	Weight	Reps
		3 x 20		3 x 20		3 x 20		3 x 20

EXAMPLE: PRE-SEASON STRENGTH & CONDITIONING: WEEKS 5 - 8								
							1 Rep Max	Week
DAY 2	WEEK 5		WEEK 6		WEEK 7		WEEK 8	
	Weight	Reps	Weight	Reps	Weight	Reps	Weight	Reps
Squats	25-45 lbs.	12	25-45 lbs.	12	25-45 lbs.	12	25-45 lbs.	12
	65%	3	65%	3	65%	3	65%	3
	67%	3	67%	3	67%	3	67%	3
	69%	3	69%	3	69%	3	69%	3
	71%	3	71%	3	71%	3	71%	3
	71%	3	71%	3	71%	3	71%	3
	73%	3	73%	3	73%	3	73%	3
	73%	3	73%	3	73%	3	73%	3
	74%	3	74%	3	74%	3	74%	3
Power Cleans	Weight	Reps	Weight	Reps	Weight	Reps	Weight	Reps
	64%	5	64%	5	64%	3	64%	3
	70%	4	70%	4	70%	3	70%	3
	73%	3	76%	3	76%	3	76%	3
	76%	3	79%	3	82%	3	82%	3
	79%	3	82%	3	88%	2	88%	2
Dumbbell Lunges *(Superset with Dumbbell Heavy Shrugs)*	Weight	Reps	Weight	Reps	Weight	Reps	Weight	Reps
		8		8		8		8
		8		8		8		8
		8		8		8		8
Dumbbell Heavy Shrugs *(Superset with Dumbbell Lunges)*	Weight	Reps	Weight	Reps	Weight	Reps	Weight	Reps
		8		8		8		8
		8		8		8		8
		8		8		8		8
Straight Leg Deadlift	Weight	Reps	Weight	Reps	Weight	Reps	Weight	Reps
		8		8		8		8
		8		8		8		8
		8		8		8		8
Lat Pulls to Front	Weight	Reps	Weight	Reps	Weight	Reps	Weight	Reps
		10		10		10		10
		10		10		10		10
		10		10		10		10
Hyper Extensions or Hamstring Curls *(Superset with Crunches)*	Weight	Reps	Weight	Reps	Weight	Reps	Weight	Reps
		10		10		10		10
		10		10		10		10
		10		10		10		10
Crunches *(Superset with Hyper Extensions or Hamstring Curls)*	Weight	Reps	Weight	Reps	Weight	Reps	Weight	Reps
		4 x 50		4 x 50		4 x 60		4 x 60

EXAMPLE: PRE-SEASON STRENGTH & CONDITIONING: WEEKS 5 - 8								
							Max	Week
Day 3	WEEK 5		WEEK 6		WEEK 7		WEEK 8	
Close-grip Bench Press *(Grip mid-finger at rough of bar)*	Weight	Reps	Weight	Reps	Weight	Reps	Weight	Reps
	Warm-up		Warm-up		Warm-up		Warm-up	
	65%	8	67%	8	67%	6	69%	5
Note: Subtract 25-50 lbs. from Bench Press percentages.	70%	5	69%	5	70%	5	71%	4
	76%	5	73%	5	76%	4	76%	4
	79%	5	79%	4	82%	4	82%	3
	85%	4	88%	4	88%	3	88%	3
Deadlifts	Weight	Reps	Weight	Reps	Weight	Reps	Weight	Reps
		10		10		10		10
		10		10		10		10
		10		10		10		10
Dumbbell Front Raise *(Superset with Dumbbell Side Raise)*	Weight	Reps	Weight	Reps	Weight	Reps	Weight	Reps
		10		10		10		10
		10		10		10		10
		10		10		10		10
Dumbbell Side Raise *(Superset with Dumbbell Front Raise)*	Weight	Reps	Weight	Reps	Weight	Reps	Weight	Reps
		10		10		10		10
		10		10		10		10
		10		10		10		10
Standing Barbell Tricep Extensions *(Superset with Hanging Leg Raises or Leg Lifts)*	Weight	Reps	Weight	Reps	Weight	Reps	Weight	Reps
		10		10		10		10
		10		10		10		10
		10		10		10		10
Hanging Leg Raises or Leg Lifts *(Superset with Standing Barbell Tricep Extensions)*	Weight	Reps	Weight	Reps	Weight	Reps	Weight	Reps
		3 x 25		3 x 25		3 x 25		3 x 25

*WEEK #9: ACADEMIC EXAM WEEK or REST WEEK

EXAMPLE: PRE-SEASON STRENGTH & CONDITIONING: WEEKS 10 - 15												
DAY 1	WEEK 10		WEEK 11		WEEK 12		WEEK 13		WEEK 14		WEEK 15	
Bench Press	Weight	Reps	Weight	Reps	Weight	Reps	Weight	Reps	Weight	Reps	Weight	Reps
	55%	12	58%	10	60%	10	62%	10	58%	10	61%	10
	60%	12	63%	10	65%	8	68%	8	63%	8	65%	8
	63%	12	70%	8	73%	8	75%	5	70%	5	73%	5
	61%	12	73%	8	78%	6	79%	5	76%	5	79%	4
			65%	10	69%	10	81%	5	79%	5	79%	4
							65%	10	85%	4	88%	3
Hang Clean	Weight	Reps	Weight	Reps	Weight	Reps	Weight	Reps	Weight	Reps	Weight	Reps
	54%	6	55%	5	58%	4	61%	4	64%	3	64%	3
	59%	6	61%	5	63%	4	72%	4	70%	3	70%	3
	61%	6	66%	5	70%	4	74%	4	76%	3	76%	3
	65%	6	69%	5	74%	4	77%	4	79%	3	82%	3
									82%	3	88%	2
Dumbbell Incline Bench Press	Weight	Reps	Weight	Reps	Weight	Reps	Weight	Reps	Weight	Reps	Weight	Reps
		10		10	Up Wt.	8	Up Wt.	8	Up Wt.	6	Up Wt.	6
		10		10	Up Wt.	8	Up Wt.	8	Up Wt.	6	Up Wt.	6
		10		10	Up Wt.	8	Up Wt.	8	Up Wt.	6	Up Wt.	6
Military Power Press *(Superset with Upright Rows)*	Weight	Reps	Weight	Reps	Weight	Reps	Weight	Reps	Weight	Reps	Weight	Reps
		10		10	Up Wt.	8	Up Wt.	8	Up Wt.	6	Up Wt.	6
		10		10	Up Wt.	8	Up Wt.	8	Up Wt.	6	Up Wt.	6
		10		10	Up Wt.	8	Up Wt.	8	Up Wt.	6	Up Wt.	6
Upright Rows *(Superset with Military Power Press)*	Weight	Reps	Weight	Reps	Weight	Reps	Weight	Reps	Weight	Reps	Weight	Reps
		10		10		10		10		10		10
		10		10		10		10		10		10
		10		10		10		10		10		10
Barbell Standing Tricep Extension *(Superset with Diamond Pushups)*	Weight	Reps	Weight	Reps	Weight	Reps	Weight	Reps	Weight	Reps	Weight	Reps
		10		10		10		10		10		10
		10		10		10		10		10		10
		10		10		10		10		10		10
Diamond Push Ups *(Superset with Barbell Standing Tricep Extension)*	Weight	Reps	Weight	Reps	Weight	Reps	Weight	Reps	Weight	Reps	Weight	Reps
		10		10		10		10		10		10
		10		10		10		10		10		10
		10		10		10		10		10		10
Weighted Neck Harness	Weight	Reps	Weight	Reps	Weight	Reps	Weight	Reps	Weight	Reps	Weight	Reps
	10-25 lbs.	3 x 10	10-25 lbs.	3 x 10	10-25 lbs.	3 x 10	10-25 lbs.	3 x 10	10-25 lbs.	3 x 10	10-25 lbs.	3 x 10

EXAMPLE: PRE-SEASON STRENGTH & CONDITIONING: WEEKS 10 - 15

DAY 2	WEEK 10 Weight	Reps	WEEK 11 Weight	Reps	WEEK 12 Weight	Reps	WEEK 13 Weight	Reps	WEEK 14 Weight	Reps	WEEK 15 Weight	Reps
Squat	58%	20	61%	10	63%	10	65%	10	60%	10	60%	10
	58%	20	64%	10	66%	10	70%	8	65%	8	65%	8
	58%	20	70%	10	73%	8	77%	8	70%	3	70%	3
			74%	10	80%	6	83%	6	75%	3	75%	3
			65%	10	68%	10	72%	10	80%	3	80%	3
			63%	10	65%	10	68%	10	80%	3	80%	3
									80%	3	80%	3
									80%	3	80%	3
Power Clean	54%	6	55%	5	58%	4	61%	4	64%	5	64%	5
	59%	6	61%	5	65%	4	71%	4	70%	4	70%	4
	61%	6	67%	5	71%	4	75%	4	73%	3	76%	3
	65%	6	70%	5	74%	4	78%	4	76%	3	79%	3
									79%	3	82%	3
									82%	3	85%	2
Dumbbell Lunges *(Superset with Dumbbell Straight Leg Deadlifts)*		10		8		8		8		6		6
		10		8		8		8		6		6
		10		8		8		8		6		6
Dumbbell Straight Leg Deadlifts *(Superset with Dumbbell Lunges)*		10		8		8		8		8		8
		10		8		8		8		8		8
		10		8		8		8		8		8
Hyper Extension or Hamstring Curls *(Superset with Lat Pulls)*		10		10		10		10		10		10
		10		10		10		10		10		10
		10		10		10		10		10		10
Lat Pulls to Front *(Superset with Hyper Extension or Hamstring Curls)*		10		10		10		10		10		10
		10		10		10		10		10		10
		10		10		10		10		10		10
Weighted Abdominal Twist *(Superset with Leg Up Crunches)*		3 x 15		3 x 15		3 x 15		3 x 15				
Leg Up Crunches *(Superset with Weighted Abdominal Twists)*		4 x 25		4 x 25		4 x 25		4 x 25				

EXAMPLE: PRE-SEASON STRENGTH & CONDITIONING: WEEKS 10 - 15

Day 3	WEEK 10		WEEK 11		WEEK 12		WEEK 13		WEEK 14		WEEK 15	
Incline Press	Weight	Reps	Weight	Reps	Weight	Reps	Weight	Reps	Weight	Reps	Weight	Reps
	55%	12	58%	10	65%	8	67%	8	67%	6	69%	5
	60%	12	63%	10	70%	5	69%	5	70%	5	71%	4
	63%	12	70%	8	76%	5	73%	5	76%	4	76%	4
	61%	12	73%	8	79%	5	79%	4	82%	4	82%	3
			65%	10	85%	4	88%	4	88%	3	88%	3
Deadlifts	Weight	Reps	Weight	Reps	Weight	Reps	Weight	Reps	Weight	Reps	Weight	Reps
	61%	10	63%	10	65%	10	68%	10	70%	5	70%	5
	64%	10	69%	10	72%	8	75%	8	79%	4	80%	3
	70%	10	73%	8	77%	8	80%	6	82%	4	85%	2
	67%	10	77%	6	81%	6	83%	6	85%	3	90%	1
Weighted Chair Dips *(Superset with Heavy Shrugs)*	Weight	Reps	Weight	Reps	Weight	Reps	Weight	Reps	Weight	Reps	Weight	Reps
		10		10		10		10		10		10
		10		10		10		10		10		10
		10		10		10		10		10		10
Heavy Shrugs *(Superset with Weighted Chair Dips)*	Weight	Reps	Weight	Reps	Weight	Reps	Weight	Reps	Weight	Reps	Weight	Reps
		10		10		10		10		10		10
		10		10		10		10		10		10
		10		10		10		10		10		10
Good Mornings *(Superset with Hanging Leg Raises or Leg Lifts)*	Weight	Reps	Weight	Reps	Weight	Reps	Weight	Reps	Weight	Reps	Weight	Reps
		10		10		10		10		10		10
		10		10		10		10		10		10
		10		10		10		10		10		10
Hanging Leg Raises or Leg Lifts *(Super Set with Good Mornings)*	Weight	Reps	Weight	Reps	Weight	Reps	Weight	Reps	Weight	Reps	Weight	Reps
		4 x 25		4 x 25		4 x 25		4 x 25		4 x 25		4 x 25

EXAMPLE: SUMMER STRENGTH & CONDITIONING: WEEKS 1 - 6

WEEK #1 - MONDAY

NOTES	3 areas, 15 min rotation.				
	Group 1 Students	**Group 2 Students**	**Group 3 Students**	**Group 4 Students**	**Group 5 Students**
AREA 1	**Rack 1**	**Rack 2**	**Rack 3**	**Rack 4**	**Rack 5**
Exercise	Barbell Incline Bench Press	Barbell Incline Bench Press	Barbell Incline Bench Press	Barbell Incline Bench Press	Barbell Incline Bench Press
Sets x Reps	3 x 8-10	3 x 8-10	3 x 8-10	3 x 8-10	3 x 8-10
AREA 2	**Platform**	**Platform**	**Platform**	**Platform**	**Platform**
Exercise	Barbell Shrugs	Barbell Shrugs	Barbell Shrugs	Barbell Low Row	Barbell Low Row
Sets x Reps	3 x 8-10	3 x 8-10	3 x 8-10	3 x 8-10	3 x 8-10
AREA 3A	**Dumbbell Racks**	**Dumbbell Racks**	**Dumbbell Racks**	**Dumbbell Racks**	**Dumbbell Racks**
Exercise	Barbell / Dumbbell Upright Row	Barbell / Dumbbell Upright Row	Barbell / Dumbbell Bicep Curls	Barbell / Dumbbell Bicep Curls	Barbell / Dumbbell Bicep Curls
Sets x Reps	2 x 8-10	2 x 8-10	2 x 8-10	2 x 8-10	2 x 8-10

AREA 3B	Machine Area	Machine Area	Machine Area	Machine Area	Machine Area
Exercise	Lat Pulls	Full sit ups	Triceps Pushdown	Straight leg raises	Neck Push
Sets x Reps	2 x 8-10	2 x 8-10	2 x 8-10	2 x 8-10	2 x 8-10

EXAMPLE: SUMMER STRENGTH & CONDITIONING: WEEKS 1 - 6
WEEK #1 - TUESDAY

NOTES	3 areas, 15 min rotation.				
	Group 1 Students	Group 2 Students	Group 3 Students	Group 4 Students	Group 5 Students
AREA 1	Rack 1	Rack 2	Rack 3	Rack 4	Rack 5
Exercise	Barbell Squat	Barbell Squat	Barbell Squat	Barbell Squat	Barbell Squat
Sets x Reps	3 x 8-10	3 x 8-10	3 x 8-10	3 x 8-10	3 x 8-10
AREA 2	Platform	Platform	Platform	Platform	Platform
Exercise	Barbell Deadlift	Barbell Deadlift	Barbell Deadlift	Barbell Deadlift	Barbell Deadlift
Sets x Reps	3 x 8-10	3 x 8-10	3 x 8-10	3 x 8-10	3 x 8-10
AREA 3A	Dumbbell Racks	Dumbbell Racks	Dumbbell Racks	Dumbbell Racks	Dumbbell Racks
Exercise	Barbell / Dumbbell Step Ups	Barbell / Dumbbell Step Ups	Barbell Lat Lunge	Barbell Lat Lunge	Barbell Lat Lunge
Sets x Reps	2 x 8-10	2 x 8-10	2 x 8-10	2 x 8-10	2 x 8-10
AREA 3B	Machine Area	Machine Area	Machine Area	Machine Area	Machine Area
Exercise	Hamstring Curls	Leg Extensions	Front Planks	Front Plank Twists or Side Planks	Neck Back Push
Sets x Reps	2 x 8-10	2 x 8-10	2 x 8-10	2 x 8-10	2 x 8-10

EXAMPLE: SUMMER STRENGTH & CONDITIONING: WEEKS 1 - 6
WEEK #1 - WEDNESDAY

NOTES	3 areas, 15 min rotation.				
	Group 1 Students	Group 2 Students	Group 3 Students	Group 4 Students	Group 5 Students
AREA 1	Rack 1	Rack 2	Rack 3	Rack 4	Rack 5
Exercise	Barbell Incline	Barbell Incline	Barbell Incline	Close-grip Bench Press	Close-grip Bench Press
Sets x Reps	3 x 8-10	3 x 8-10	3 x 8-10	3 x 8-10	3 x 8-10
AREA 1	Rack 6 (Smith Machine)				
Exercise	Close-grip Bench Press				
Sets x Reps	3 x 8-10				
AREA 2	Pl32atform	Platform	Platform	Platform	Platform
Exercise	Barbell Shrugs	Barbell Shrugs	Barbell Shrugs	Barbell Low Row	Barbell Low Row
Sets x Reps	3 x 8-10	3 x 8-10	3 x 8-10	3 x 8-10	3 x 8-10
AREA 3A	Dumbbell Racks	Dumbbell Racks	Dumbbell Racks	Dumbbell Racks	Dumbbell Racks
Exercise	Barbell / Dumbbell Upright Rows	Barbell / Dumbbell Upright Rows	Dumbbell Back Rows	Dumbbell Back Rows	Dumbbell Side Raise
Sets x Reps	2 x 8-10	2 x 8-10	2 x 8-10	2 x 8-10	2 x 8-10
AREA 3A	Machine Area	Dumbbell Racks	Dumbbell Racks		
Exercise	Dumbbell Side Raise	Dumbbell Rear Raise	Dumbbell Rear Raise		

Sets x Reps	2 x 8-10	2 x 8-10	2 x 8-10		
AREA 3B	Machine Area	Machine Area	Machine Area	Machine Area	Machine Area
Exercise	Russian Twist	Triangle Crunch	Wide Leg Crunch	Neck Rt Side	
Sets x Reps	2 x 8-10	2 x 8-10	2 x 8-10	2 x 8-10	

EXAMPLE: SUMMER STRENGTH & CONDITIONING: WEEKS 1 - 6
WEEK #1 - THURSDAY

NOTES	3 areas, 15 min rotation.				
	Group 1 Students	Group 2 Students	Group 3 Students	Group 4 Students	Group 5 Students
AREA 1	Rack 1	Rack 2	Rack 3	Rack 4	Rack 5
Exercise	Front Squat	Front Squat	Front Squat	Front Squat	Front Squat
Sets x Reps	3 x 10-12	3 x 10-12	3 x 10-12	3 x 10-12	3 x 10-12
AREA 2	Platform	Platform	Platform	Platform	Platform
Exercise	Barbell Russian Deadlift	Barbell Russian Deadlift	Barbell Russian Deadlift	Barbell Russian Deadlift	Barbell Russian Deadlift
Sets x Reps	3 x 10-12	3 x 10-12	3 x 10-12	3 x 10-12	3 x 10-12
AREA 3A	Dumbbell Racks	Dumbbell Racks	Dumbbell Racks	Dumbbell Racks	Dumbbell Racks
Exercise	4-way Dumbbell Lunge	4-way Dumbbell Lunge	Barbell Lat Lunge	Barbell Lat Lunge	Barbell Lat Lunge
Sets x Reps	2 x 8-10	2 x 8-10	2 x 8-10	2 x 8-10	2 x 8-10
AREA 3B	Machine Area	Machine Area	Machine Area	Machine Area	Machine Area
Exercise	Hamstring Curls	Single Leg Press	Bicycles	V-Ups or Side Planks	Side Crunch
Sets x Reps	2 x 8-10	2 x 8-10	2 x 8-10	2 x 8-10	2 x 8-10
AREA 3C	Outside	Machine Area			
Exercise	Walking Lunges	Neck LF Side			
Sets x Reps	2 x 8-10	2 x 8-10			

EXAMPLE: SUMMER STRENGTH & CONDITIONING: WEEKS 1 - 6
WEEK #2 - MONDAY

NOTES	3 areas, 15 min rotation.				
	Group 1 Students	Group 2 Students	Group 3 Students	Group 4 Students	Group 5 Students
AREA 1	Rack 1	Rack 2	Rack 3	Rack 4	Rack 5
Exercise	Barbell Incline	Barbell Incline	Barbell Incline	Barbell Incline	Barbell Incline
Sets x Reps	63% x 8 65% x 6 70% x 6 75% x 5 78% x 5	63% x 8 65% x 6 70% x 6 75% x 5 78% x 5	63% x 8 65% x 6 70% x 6 75% x 5 78% x 5	63% x 8 65% x 6 70% x 6 75% x 5 78% x 5	63% x 8 65% x 6 70% x 6 75% x 5 78% x 5
AREA 2	Platform	Platform	Platform	Platform	Platform
Exercise	Barbell Heavy Shrugs	Barbell Heavy Shrugs	Barbell Heavy Shrugs	Barbell Heavy Shrugs	Barbell Heavy Shrugs
Sets x Reps	3 x 8	3 x 8	3 x 8	3 x 8	3 x 8
AREA 3A	Dumbbell Racks	Dumbbell Racks	Dumbbell Racks	Dumbbell Racks	Dumbbell Racks
Exercise	Barbell / Dumbbell Upright Rows	Barbell / Dumbbell Upright Rows	Barbell / Dumbbell Bicep Curls	Barbell / Dumbbell Bicep Curls	Barbell / Dumbbell Bicep Curls
Sets x Reps	2 x 8-10	2 x 8-10	2 x 8-10	2 x 8-10	2 x 8-10
AREA 3B	Machine Area	Machine Area	Machine Area	Machine Area	Machine Area

Exercise	Lat Pulls	Full Sit Ups	Tricep Pushdown	Straight Leg Raises or Wipers- Slight Bend	Neck Front Push
Sets x Reps	2 x 8-10	2 x 8-10	2 x 8-10	2 x 8-10	2 x 8-10

EXAMPLE: SUMMER STRENGTH & CONDITIONING: WEEKS 1 - 6
WEEK #2 - TUESDAY

NOTES	3 areas, 15 min rotation.				
	Group 1 Students	Group 2 Students	Group 3 Students	Group 4 Students	Group 5 Students
AREA 1	Rack 1	Rack 2	Rack 3	Rack 4	Rack 5
Exercise	Barbell Squat	Barbell Squat	Barbell Squat	Barbell Squat	Barbell Squat
Sets x Reps	60% x 10 63% x 8 68% x 6 73% x 5 75% x 5	60% x 10 63% x 8 68% x 6 73% x 5 75% x 5	60% x 10 63% x 8 68% x 6 73% x 5 75% x 5	60% x 10 63% x 8 68% x 6 73% x 5 75% x 5	60% x 10 63% x 8 68% x 6 73% x 5 75% x 5
AREA 2	Platform	Platform	Platform	Platform	Platform
Exercise	Heavy Barbell Deadlift	Heavy Barbell Deadlift	Heavy Barbell Deadlift	Heavy Barbell Deadlift	Heavy Barbell Deadlift
Sets x Reps	4 x 8	4 x 8	4 x 8	4 x 8	4 x 8
AREA 3A	Dumbbell Racks	Dumbbell Racks	Dumbbell Racks	Dumbbell Racks	Dumbbell Racks
Exercise	Barbell / Dumbbell Step Ups	Barbell / Dumbbell Step Ups	Barbell Lateral Lunge	Barbell Lateral Lunge	Barbell Lateral Lunge
Sets x Reps	2 x 8-10	2 x 8-10	2 x 8-10	2 x 8-10	2 x 8-10
AREA 3B	Machine Area	Machine Area	Machine Area	Machine Area	Machine Area
Exercise	Hamstring Curls	Leg Extensions	Front Planks	Side Planks	Neck Push
Sets x Reps	2 x 8-10	2 x 8-10	2 x 8-10	2 x 8-10	2 x 8-10

EXAMPLE: SUMMER STRENGTH & CONDITIONING: WEEKS 1 - 6
WEEK #2 - WEDNESDAY

NOTES	3 areas, 15 min rotation.				
	Group 1 Students	Group 2 Students	Group 3 Students	Group 4 Students	Group 5 Students
AREA 1	Rack 1	Rack 2	Rack 3	Rack 4	Rack 5
Exercise	Barbell Incline	Barbell Incline	Barbell Incline	Barbell Incline	Barbell Incline
Sets x Reps	3 x 8-10	3 x 8-10	3 x 8-10	3 x 8-10	3 x 8-10
AREA 1	Smith Machine				
Exercise	Close Grip Bench Press				
Sets x Reps	3 x 8-10				
AREA 2	Platform	Platform	Platform	Platform	Platform
Exercise	Barbell Shrugs	Barbell Shrugs	Barbell Shrugs	Barbell Low Row	Barbell Low Row
Sets x Reps	3 x 8-10	3 x 8-10	3 x 8-10	3 x 8-10	3 x 8-10
AREA 3A	Dumbbell Racks	Dumbbell Racks	Dumbbell Racks	Dumbbell Racks	Dumbbell Racks
Exercise	Barbell / Dumbbell Upright Rows	Barbell / Dumbbell Upright Rows	Dumbbell Back Rows	Dumbbell Back Rows	Dumbbell Side Raises
Sets x Reps	2 x 8-10	2 x 8-10	2 x 8-10	2 x 8-10	2 x 8-10

AREA 3B	Machine Area	Machine Area	Machine Area	Machine Area	Machine Area
Exercise	Dumbbell Side Raise	Dumbbell Rear Raise	Dumbbell Rear Raise		
Sets x Reps	2 x 8-10	2 x 8-10	2 x 8-10		
AREA 3B	Machine Area	Machine Area	Machine Area	Machine Area	Machine Area
Exercise	Russian Twist	Triangle Crunch	Wide Leg Crunch	Neck Right Side	
Sets x Reps	2 x 8-10	2 x 8-10	2 x 8-10	2 x 8-10	

EXAMPLE: SUMMER STRENGTH & CONDITIONING: WEEKS 1 - 6					
WEEK #2 - THURSDAY					
NOTES	3 areas, 15 min rotation.				
	Group 1 Students	Group 2 Students	Group 3 Students	Group 4 Students	Group 5 Students
AREA 1	Rack 1	Rack 2	Rack 3	Rack 4	Rack 5
Exercise	Front Squat	Front Squat	Front Squat	Front Squat	Front Squat
Sets x Reps	3 x 8-10	3 x 8-10	3 x 8-10	3 x 8-10	3 x 8-10
AREA 2	Platform	Platform	Platform	Platform	Platform
Exercise	Barbell Russian Deadlift	Barbell Russian Deadlift	Barbell Russian Deadlift	Barbell Russian Deadlift	Barbell Russian Deadlift
Sets x Reps	3 x 8-10	3 x 8-10	3 x 8-10	3 x 8-10	3 x 8-10
AREA 3A	Dumbbell Racks	Dumbbell Racks	Dumbbell Racks	Dumbbell Racks	Dumbbell Racks
Exercise	4-way Dumbbell Lunge	4-way Dumbbell Lunge	Barbell Lateral Lunge	Barbell Lateral Lunge	Barbell Lateral Lunge
Sets x Reps	2 x 8-10	2 x 8-10	2 x 8-10	2 x 8-10	2 x 8-10
AREA 3B	Machine Area	Machine Area	Machine Area	Machine Area	Machine Area
Exercise	Hamstring Curls	Single Leg Press	Bicycles	V-Ups or Side Planks	Side Crunch
Sets x Reps	2 x 8-10	2 x 8-10	2 x 8-10	2 x 8-10	2 x 8-10
AREA 3C	Outside	Machine Area	Machine Area	Machine Area	Machine Area
Exercise	Walking Lunge	Neck Lf Side			
Sets x Reps	2 x 8-10	2 x 8-10			

EXAMPLE: SUMMER STRENGTH & CONDITIONING: WEEKS 1 - 6					
WEEK #3 - MONDAY					
NOTES	3 areas, 15 min rotation.				
	Group 1 Students	Group 2 Students	Group 3 Students	Group 4 Students	Group 5 Students
AREA 1	Rack 1	Rack 2	Rack 3	Rack 4	Rack 5
Exercise	Barbell Incline	Barbell Incline	Barbell Incline	Barbell Incline	Barbell Incline
Sets x Reps	68% x 8 73% x 5 76% x 5 78% x 5 78% x 5	68% x 8 73% x 5 76% x 5 78% x 5 78% x 5	68% x 8 73% x 5 76% x 5 78% x 5 78% x 5	68% x 8 73% x 5 76% x 5 78% x 5 78% x 5	68% x 8 73% x 5 76% x 5 78% x 5 78% x 5
AREA 2	Platform	Platform	Platform	Platform	Platform
Exercise	Heavy Barbell Shrugs	Heavy Barbell Shrugs	Heavy Barbell Shrugs	Heavy Barbell Shrugs	Heavy Barbell Shrugs
Sets x Reps	4 x 8	4 x 8	4 x 8	4 x 8	4 x 8
AREA 3A	Dumbbell Racks	Dumbbell Racks	Dumbbell Racks	Dumbbell Racks	Dumbbell Racks
Exercise	Barbell / Dumbbell Upright	Barbell / Dumbbell Upright	Barbell / Dumbbell Bicep	Barbell / Dumbbell Bicep	Barbell / Dumbbell Bicep Curls

	Rows	Rows	Curls	Curls	
Sets x Reps	2 x 8-10	2 x 8-10	2 x 8-10	2 x 8-10	2 x 8-10
AREA 3B	**Machine Area**	**Machine Area**	**Machine Area**	**Machine Area**	**Machine Area**
Exercise	Lat Pulls	Full Sit Ups	Triceps Pushdown	Straight Leg Raises	Neck Front Push
Sets x Reps	2 x 8-10	2 x 8-10	2 x 8-10	2 x 8-10	2 x 8-10

EXAMPLE: SUMMER STRENGTH & CONDITIONING: WEEKS 1 - 6					
WEEK #3 - TUESDAY					
NOTES	3 areas, 15 min rotation.				
	Group 1 Students	**Group 2 Students**	**Group 3 Students**	**Group 4 Students**	**Group 5 Students**
AREA 1	**Rack 1**	**Rack 2**	**Rack 3**	**Rack 4**	**Rack 5**
Exercise	Barbell Squat	Barbell Squat	Barbell Squat	Barbell Squat	Barbell Squat
Sets x Reps	63% x 8 68% x 6 73% x 5 75% x 5 78% x 5	63% x 8 68% x 6 73% x 5 75% x 5 78% x 5	63% x 8 68% x 6 73% x 5 75% x 5 78% x 5	63% x 8 68% x 6 73% x 5 75% x 5 78% x 5	63% x 8 68% x 6 73% x 5 75% x 5 78% x 5
AREA 2	**Platform**	**Platform**	**Platform**	**Platform**	**Platform**
Exercise	Heavy Barbell Deadlift	Heavy Barbell Deadlift	Heavy Barbell Deadlift	Heavy Barbell Deadlift	Heavy Barbell Deadlift
Sets x Reps	4 x 8	4 x 8	4 x 8	4 x 8	4 x 8
AREA 3A	**Dumbbell Racks**	**Dumbbell Racks**	**Dumbbell Racks**	**Dumbbell Racks**	**Dumbbell Racks**
Exercise	Barbell / Dumbbell Step Ups	Barbell / Dumbbell Step Ups	Barbell Lateral Lunge	Barbell Lateral Lunge	Barbell Lateral Lunge
Sets x Reps	2 x 8-10	2 x 8-10	2 x 8-10	2 x 8-10	2 x 8-10
AREA 3B	**Machine Area**	**Machine Area**	**Machine Area**	**Machine Area**	**Machine Area**
Exercise	Hamstring Curls	Leg Extensions	Front Planks	Front Plank Twist or Side Planks	Neck Back Push
Sets x Reps	2 x 8-10	2 x 8-10	2 x 8-10	2 x 8-10	2 x 8-10

EXAMPLE: SUMMER STRENGTH & CONDITIONING: WEEKS 1 - 6					
WEEK 3 - WEDNESDAY					
NOTES	3 areas, 15 min rotation.				
	Group 1 Students	**Group 2 Students**	**Group 3 Students**	**Group 4 Students**	**Group 5 Students**
AREA 1	**Rack 1**	**Rack 2**	**Rack 3**	**Rack 4**	**Rack 5**
Exercise	Barbell Incline	Barbell Squat	Barbell Squat	Close Grip Bench Press	Close Grip Bench Press
Sets x Reps	63% x 8 73% x 5 76% x 5 78% x 5 78% x 5	63% x 8 73% x 5 76% x 5 78% x 5 78% x 5	63% x 8 73% x 5 76% x 5 78% x 5 78% x 5	4 x 8	4 x 8
AREA 1	**Rack 6 (Smith Machine)**				
Exercise	Close Grip Bench Press				
Sets x Reps	4 x 8				

AREA 2	Platform	Platform	Platform	Platform	Platform
Exercise	Barbell Shrugs	Barbell Shrugs	Barbell Shrugs	Barbell Low Row	Barbell Low Row
Sets x Reps	5 x 8	5 x 8	5 x 8	5 x 8	5 x 8
AREA 3A	**Dumbbell Racks**	**Dumbbell Racks**	**Dumbbell Racks**	**Dumbbell Racks**	**Dumbbell Racks**
Exercise	Barbell / Dumbbell Upright Row	Barbell / Dumbbell Upright Row	Dumbbell Back Row	Dumbbell Back Row	Dumbbell Side Raise
Sets x Reps	2 x 8-10	2 x 8-10	2 x 8-10	2 x 8-10	2 x 8-10
AREA 3B	**Machine Area**	**Machine Area**	**Machine Area**	**Machine Area**	**Machine Area**
Exercise	Dumbbell Side Raise	Dumbbell Rear Raise	Dumbbell Rear Raise		
Sets x Reps	2 x 8-10	2 x 8-10	2 x 8-10		
AREA 3B	**Machine Area**	**Machine Area**	**Machine Area**	**Machine Area**	**Machine Area**
Exercise	Russian Twists	Triangle Crunch	Wide Leg Crunch	Neck RT Side	
Sets x Reps	2 x 10-25	2 x 10-25	2 x 10-25	2 x 8-10	

EXAMPLE: SUMMER STRENGTH & CONDITIONING: WEEKS 1 - 6					
WEEK 3 - THURSDAY					
NOTES	3 areas, 15 min rotation.				
	Group 1 Students	**Group 2 Students**	**Group 3 Students**	**Group 4 Students**	**Group 5 Students**
AREA 1	**Rack 1**	**Rack 2**	**Rack 3**	**Rack 4**	**Rack 5**
Exercise	Front Squat	Front Squat	Front Squat	Front Squat	Front Squat
Sets x Reps	3 x 10-12	3 x 10-12	3 x 10-12	3 x 10-12	3 x 10-12
AREA 2	**Platform**	**Platform**	**Platform**	**Platform**	**Platform**
Exercise	Barbell Russian Deadlift	Barbell Russian Deadlift	Barbell Deadlift	Barbell Deadlift	Barbell Deadlift
Sets x Reps	4 x 8	4 x 8	4 x 8	4 x 8	4 x 8
AREA 3A	**Dumbbell Racks**	**Dumbbell Racks**	**Dumbbell Racks**	**Dumbbell Racks**	**Dumbbell Racks**
Exercise	4-way Dumbbell Lunge	4-way Dumbbell Lunge	Barbell Lateral Lunge	Barbell Lateral Lunge	Barbell Lateral Lunge
Sets x Reps	2 x 8-10	2 x 8-10	2 x 8-10	2 x 8-10	2 x 8-10
AREA 3B	**Machine Area**	**Machine Area**	**Machine Area**	**Machine Area**	**Machine Area**
Exercise	Hamstring Curls	Single Leg Press	Bicycles	V-Ups or Side Planks	Side Crunch
Sets x Reps	2 x 8-10	2 x 8-10	2 x 8-10	2 x 8-10	2 x 8-10
AREA 3C	**Outside**	**Machine Area**			
Exercise	Walking Lunge	Neck LF Side			
Sets x Reps	2 x 8-10	2 x 8-10			

EXAMPLE: SUMMER STRENGTH & CONDITIONING: WEEKS 1 - 6					
WEEK 4 - MONDAY					
NOTES	3 areas, 15 min rotation.				
	Group 1 Students	**Group 2 Students**	**Group 3 Students**	**Group 4 Students**	**Group 5 Students**
AREA 1	**Rack 1**	**Rack 2**	**Rack 3**	**Rack 4**	**Rack 5**
Exercise	Barbell Incline	Barbell Incline	Barbell Incline	Barbell Incline	Barbell Incline
Sets x Reps	68% x 8 73% x 6	68% x 8 73% x 6	68% x 8 73% x 6	68% x 8 73% x 6	68% x 8 73% x 6

	Group 1 Students	Group 2 Students	Group 3 Students	Group 4 Students	Group 5 Students
	76% x 5 80% x 4 88% x 2	76% x 5 80% x 4 88% x 2	76% x 5 80% x 4 88% x 2	76% x 5 80% x 4 88% x 2	76% x 5 80% x 4 88% x 2
AREA 2	**Platform**	**Platform**	**Platform**	**Platform**	**Platform**
Exercise	Heavy Barbell Shrugs	Heavy Barbell Shrugs	Heavy Barbell Shrugs	Heavy Barbell Shrugs	Heavy Barbell Shrugs
Sets x Reps	5 x 8	5 x 8	5 x 8	5 x 8	5 x 8
AREA 3A	**Dumbbell Racks**	**Dumbbell Racks**	**Dumbbell Racks**	**Dumbbell Racks**	**Dumbbell Racks**
Exercise	Barbell / Dumbbell Upright Rows	Barbell / Dumbbell Upright Rows	Barbell / Dumbbell Bicep Curls	Barbell / Dumbbell Bicep Curls	Barbell / Dumbbell Bicep Curls
Sets x Reps	2 x 8-10	2 x 8-10	2 x 8-10	2 x 8-10	2 x 8-10
AREA 3B	**Machine Area**	**Machine Area**	**Machine Area**	**Machine Area**	**Machine Area**
Exercise	Lat Pulls	Full Sit Ups	Triceps Pushdown	Straight Leg Raises	Neck Front Push
Sets x Reps	2 x 8-10	2 x 8-10	2 x 8-10	2 x 8-10	2 x 8-10

EXAMPLE: SUMMER STRENGTH & CONDITIONING: WEEKS 1 - 6					
WEEK 4 - TUESDAY					
NOTES	3 areas, 15 min rotation.				
	Group 1 Students	**Group 2 Students**	**Group 3 Students**	**Group 4 Students**	**Group 5 Students**
AREA 1	**Rack 1**	**Rack 2**	**Rack 3**	**Rack 4**	**Rack 5**
Exercise	Barbell Squat	Barbell Squat	Barbell Squat	Barbell Squat	Barbell Squat
Sets x Reps	63% x 8 68% x 6 73% x 5 75% x 5 78% x 5	63% x 8 68% x 6 73% x 5 75% x 5 78% x 5	63% x 8 68% x 6 73% x 5 75% x 5 78% x 5	63% x 8 68% x 6 73% x 5 75% x 5 78% x 5	63% x 8 68% x 6 73% x 5 75% x 5 78% x 5
AREA 2	**Platform**	**Platform**	**Platform**	**Platform**	**Platform**
Exercise	Heavy Barbell Deadlift	Heavy Barbell Deadlift	Heavy Barbell Deadlift	Heavy Barbell Deadlift	Heavy Barbell Deadlift
Sets x Reps	5 x 8	5 x 8	5 x 8	5 x 8	5 x 8
AREA 3A	**Dumbbell Racks**	**Dumbbell Racks**	**Dumbbell Racks**	**Dumbbell Racks**	**Dumbbell Racks**
Exercise	Barbell / Dumbbell Step Ups	Barbell / Dumbbell Step Ups	Barbell Lateral Lunge	Barbell Lateral Lunge	Barbell Lateral Lunge
Sets x Reps	2 x 8-10	2 x 8-10	2 x 8-10	2 x 8-10	2 x 8-10
AREA 3B	**Machine Area**	**Machine Area**	**Machine Area**	**Machine Area**	**Machine Area**
Exercise	Hamstring Curls	Leg Extensions	Front Planks	Front Plank Twist or Side Planks	Neck Back Push
Sets x Reps	2 x 8-10	2 x 8-10	2 x 8-10	2 x 8-10	2 x 8-10

EXAMPLE: SUMMER STRENGTH & CONDITIONING: WEEKS 1 - 6					
WEEK 4 - WEDNESDAY					
NOTES	3 areas, 15 min rotation.				
	Group 1 Students	**Group 2 Students**	**Group 3 Students**	**Group 4 Students**	**Group 5 Students**
AREA 1	**Rack 1**	**Rack 2**	**Rack 3**	**Rack 4**	**Rack 5**
Exercise	Barbell Incline	Barbell Squat	Barbell Squat	Close Grip Bench Press	Close Grip Bench Press

	Group 1	Group 2	Group 3	Group 4	Group 5
Sets x Reps	68% x 8 73% x 5 76% x 5 78% x 5 83% x 3	68% x 8 73% x 5 76% x 5 78% x 5 83% x 3	68% x 8 73% x 5 76% x 5 78% x 5 83% x 3	5 x 8 Add weight	5 x 8 Add weight
AREA 1	**Rack 6 (Smith Machine)**				
Exercise	Close Grip Bench Press				
Sets x Reps	5 x 6				
AREA 2	**Platform**	**Platform**	**Platform**	**Platform**	**Platform**
Exercise	Barbell Shrugs	Barbell Shrugs	Barbell Shrugs	Barbell Low Row	Barbell Low Row
Sets x Reps	5 x 8	5 x 8	5 x 8	5 x 8	5 x 8
AREA 3A	**Dumbbell Racks**	**Dumbbell Racks**	**Dumbbell Racks**	**Dumbbell Racks**	**Dumbbell Racks**
Exercise	Barbell / Dumbbell Upright Row	Barbell / Dumbbell Upright Row	Dumbbell Back Row	Dumbbell Back Row	Dumbbell Side Raise
Sets x Reps	2 x 8-10	2 x 8-10	2 x 8-10	2 x 8-10	2 x 8-10
AREA 3B	**Machine Area**	**Machine Area**	**Machine Area**	**Machine Area**	**Machine Area**
Exercise	Dumbbell Side Raise	Dumbbell Rear Raise	Dumbbell Rear Raise		
Sets x Reps	2 x 8-10	2 x 8-10	2 x 8-10		
AREA 3B	**Machine Area**	**Machine Area**	**Machine Area**	**Machine Area**	**Machine Area**
Exercise	Russian Twists	Triangle Crunch	Wide Leg Crunch	Neck RT Side	
Sets x Reps	2 x 10-25	2 x 10-25	2 x 10-25	2 x 8-10	

EXAMPLE: SUMMER STRENGTH & CONDITIONING: WEEKS 1 - 6					
WEEK 4 - THURSDAY					
NOTES	3 areas, 15 min rotation.				
	Group 1 Students	**Group 2 Students**	**Group 3 Students**	**Group 4 Students**	**Group 5 Students**
AREA 1	**Rack 1**	**Rack 2**	**Rack 3**	**Rack 4**	**Rack 5**
Exercise	Front Squat	Barbell Squat	Barbell Squat	Barbell Squat	Barbell Squat
Sets x Reps	63% x 8 68% x 8 73% x 6 73% x 5 73% x 5	63% x 8 68% x 8 73% x 6 73% x 5 73% x 5	63% x 8 68% x 8 73% x 6 73% x 5 73% x 5	63% x 8 68% x 8 73% x 6 73% x 5 73% x 5	63% x 8 68% x 8 73% x 6 73% x 5 73% x 5
AREA 2	**Platform**	**Platform**	**Platform**	**Platform**	**Platform**
Exercise	Heavy Barbell Deadlift	Heavy Barbell Deadlift	Heavy Barbell Deadlift	Heavy Barbell Deadlift	Heavy Barbell Deadlift
Sets x Reps	5 x 8	5 x 8	5 x 8	5 x 8	5 x 8
AREA 3A	**Dumbbell Racks**	**Dumbbell Racks**	**Dumbbell Racks**	**Dumbbell Racks**	**Dumbbell Racks**
Exercise	Barbell / Dumbbell Step Ups	Barbell / Dumbbell Step Ups	Barbell Lateral Lunge	Barbell Lateral Lunge	Barbell Lateral Lunge
Sets x Reps	2 x 10	2 x 10	2 x 10	2 x 10	2 x 10
AREA 3B	**Machine Area**	**Machine Area**	**Machine Area**	**Machine Area**	**Machine Area**
Exercise	Hamstring Curls	Leg Extensions	Front Planks	Front Plank Twists or Side Planks	Neck Back Push

Sets x Reps	2 x 10	2 x 10	2 x 10	2 x 10	2 x 10
AREA 3C	**Outside**	**Machine Area**			
Exercise	Walking Lunge	Neck LF Side			
Sets x Reps	2 x 8-10	2 x 8-10			

EXAMPLE: SUMMER STRENGTH & CONDITIONING: WEEKS 1 - 6
WEEK 5 - MONDAY

NOTES	3 areas, 15 min rotation.				
	Group 1 Students	**Group 2 Students**	**Group 3 Students**	**Group 4 Students**	**Group 5 Students**
AREA 1	**Rack 1**	**Rack 2**	**Rack 3**	**Rack 4**	**Rack 5**
Exercise	Barbell Incline	Barbell Incline	Barbell Incline	Barbell Incline	Barbell Incline
Sets x Reps	68% x 8 73% x 6 76% x 5 80% x 4 88% x 2	68% x 8 73% x 6 76% x 5 80% x 4 88% x 2	68% x 8 73% x 6 76% x 5 80% x 4 88% x 2	68% x 8 73% x 6 76% x 5 80% x 4 88% x 2	68% x 8 73% x 6 76% x 5 80% x 4 88% x 2
AREA 2	**Platform**	**Platform**	**Platform**	**Platform**	**Platform**
Exercise	Heavy Barbell Shrugs	Heavy Barbell Shrugs	Heavy Barbell Shrugs	Heavy Barbell Shrugs	Heavy Barbell Shrugs
Sets x Reps	5 x 8	5 x 8	5 x 8	5 x 8	5 x 8
AREA 3A	**Dumbbell Racks**	**Dumbbell Racks**	**Dumbbell Racks**	**Dumbbell Racks**	**Dumbbell Racks**
Exercise	Barbell / Dumbbell Upright Rows	Barbell / Dumbbell Upright Rows	Barbell / Dumbbell Bicep Curls	Barbell / Dumbbell Bicep Curls	Barbell / Dumbbell Bicep Curls
Sets x Reps	2 x 8-10	2 x 8-10	2 x 8-10	2 x 8-10	2 x 8-10
AREA 3B	**Machine Area**	**Machine Area**	**Machine Area**	**Machine Area**	**Machine Area**
Exercise	Lat Pulls	Full Sit Ups	Triceps Pushdown	Straight Leg Raises or Wipers- Slight Bend	Neck Front Push
Sets x Reps	2 x 8-10	2 x 8-10	2 x 8-10	2 x 8-10	2 x 8-10

EXAMPLE: SUMMER STRENGTH & CONDITIONING: WEEKS 1 - 6
WEEK 5 - TUESDAY

NOTES	3 areas, 15 min rotation.				
	Group 1 Students	**Group 2 Students**	**Group 3 Students**	**Group 4 Students**	**Group 5 Students**
AREA 1	**Rack 1**	**Rack 2**	**Rack 3**	**Rack 4**	**Rack 5**
Exercise	Barbell Squat	Barbell Squat	Barbell Squat	Barbell Squat	Barbell Squat
Sets x Reps	63% x 8 68% x 6 73% x 5 75% x 5 78% x 5	63% x 8 68% x 6 73% x 5 75% x 5 78% x 5	63% x 8 68% x 6 73% x 5 75% x 5 78% x 5	63% x 8 68% x 6 73% x 5 75% x 5 78% x 5	63% x 8 68% x 6 73% x 5 75% x 5 78% x 5
AREA 2	**Platform**	**Platform**	**Platform**	**Platform**	**Platform**
Exercise	Heavy Barbell Deadlift	Heavy Barbell Deadlift	Heavy Barbell Deadlift	Heavy Barbell Deadlift	Heavy Barbell Deadlift
Sets x Reps	5 x 8	5 x 8	5 x 8	5 x 8	5 x 8
AREA 3A	**Dumbbell Racks**	**Dumbbell Racks**	**Dumbbell Racks**	**Dumbbell Racks**	**Dumbbell Racks**
Exercise	Barbell /	Barbell /	Barbell Lateral	Barbell Lateral	Barbell Lateral

	Dumbbell Step Ups	Dumbbell Step Ups	Lunge	Lunge	Lunge
Sets x Reps	2 x 8-10	2 x 8-10	2 x 8-10	2 x 8-10	2 x 8-10
AREA 3B	**Machine Area**	**Machine Area**	**Machine Area**	**Machine Area**	**Machine Area**
Exercise	Hamstring Curls	Leg Extensions	Front Planks	Front Plank Twist or Side Planks	Neck Back Push
Sets x Reps	2 x 8-10	2 x 8-10	2 x 8-10	2 x 8-10	2 x 8-10

EXAMPLE: SUMMER STRENGTH & CONDITIONING: WEEKS 1 - 6					
WEEK 5 - WEDNESDAY					
NOTES	3 areas, 15 min rotation.				
	Group 1 Students	**Group 2 Students**	**Group 3 Students**	**Group 4 Students**	**Group 5 Students**
AREA 1	**Rack 1**	**Rack 2**	**Rack 3**	**Rack 4**	**Rack 5**
Exercise	Barbell Incline	Barbell Incline	Barbell Incline	Close Grip Bench Press	Close Grip Bench Press
Sets x Reps	68% x 8 73% x 5 76% x 5 80% x 4 88% x 2	68% x 8 73% x 5 76% x 5 80% x 4 88% x 2	68% x 8 73% x 5 76% x 5 80% x 4 88% x 2	5 x 5 Add weight	5 x 5 Add weight
AREA 1	**Rack 6 (Smith Machine)**				
Exercise	Close Grip Bench Press				
Sets x Reps	5 x 5				
AREA 2	**Platform**	**Platform**	**Platform**	**Platform**	**Platform**
Exercise	Barbell Shrugs	Barbell Shrugs	Barbell Shrugs	Barbell Low Row	Barbell Low Row
Sets x Reps	5 x 8	5 x 8	5 x 8	5 x 8	5 x 8
AREA 3A	**Dumbbell Racks**	**Dumbbell Racks**	**Dumbbell Racks**	**Dumbbell Racks**	**Dumbbell Racks**
Exercise	Barbell / Dumbbell Upright Row	Barbell / Dumbbell Upright Row	Dumbbell Back Row	Dumbbell Back Row	Dumbbell Side Raise
Sets x Reps	2 x 8-10	2 x 8-10	2 x 8-10	2 x 8-10	2 x 8-10
AREA 3B	**Machine Area**	**Machine Area**	**Machine Area**	**Machine Area**	**Machine Area**
Exercise	Dumbbell Side Raise	Dumbbell Rear Raise	Dumbbell Rear Raise		
Sets x Reps	2 x 8-10	2 x 8-10	2 x 8-10		
AREA 3B	**Machine Area**	**Machine Area**	**Machine Area**	**Machine Area**	**Machine Area**
Exercise	Russian Twists	Triangle Crunch	Wide Leg Crunch	Neck RT Side	
Sets x Reps	2 x 10-25	2 x 10-25	2 x 10-25	2 x 8-10	

EXAMPLE: SUMMER STRENGTH & CONDITIONING: WEEKS 1 - 6					
WEEK 5 - THURSDAY					
NOTES	3 areas, 15 min rotation.				
	Group 1 Students	**Group 2 Students**	**Group 3 Students**	**Group 4 Students**	**Group 5 Students**
AREA 1	**Rack 1**	**Rack 2**	**Rack 3**	**Rack 4**	**Rack 5**
Exercise	Front Squat	Barbell Squat	Barbell Squat	Barbell Squat	Barbell Squat

Sets x Reps	63% x 8 68% x 8 73% x 6 73% x 5 73% x 5	63% x 8 68% x 8 73% x 6 73% x 5 73% x 5	63% x 8 68% x 8 73% x 6 73% x 5 73% x 5	63% x 8 68% x 8 73% x 6 73% x 5 73% x 5	63% x 8 68% x 8 73% x 6 73% x 5 73% x 5
AREA 2	**Platform**	**Platform**	**Platform**	**Platform**	**Platform**
Exercise	Heavy Barbell Deadlift	Heavy Barbell Deadlift	Heavy Barbell Deadlift	Heavy Barbell Deadlift	Heavy Barbell Deadlift
Sets x Reps	5 x 8	5 x 8	5 x 8	5 x 8	5 x 8
AREA 3A	**Dumbbell Racks**	**Dumbbell Racks**	**Dumbbell Racks**	**Dumbbell Racks**	**Dumbbell Racks**
Exercise	Barbell / Dumbbell Step Ups	Barbell / Dumbbell Step Ups	Barbell Lateral Lunge	Barbell Lateral Lunge	Barbell Lateral Lunge
Sets x Reps	2 x 10	2 x 10	2 x 10	2 x 10	2 x 10
AREA 3B	**Machine Area**	**Machine Area**	**Machine Area**	**Machine Area**	**Machine Area**
Exercise	Hamstring Curls	Leg Extensions	Front Planks	Front Plank Twists or Side Planks	Neck Back Push
Sets x Reps	2 x 10	2 x 10	2 x 10	2 x 10	2 x 10

EXAMPLE: SUMMER STRENGTH & CONDITIONING: WEEKS 1 - 6					
WEEK 6 - MONDAY					
NOTES	3 areas, 15 min rotation.				
	Group 1 Students	**Group 2 Students**	**Group 3 Students**	**Group 4 Students**	**Group 5 Students**
AREA 1	**Rack 1**	**Rack 2**	**Rack 3**	**Rack 4**	**Rack 5**
Exercise	Barbell Incline	Barbell Incline	Barbell Incline	Barbell Incline	Barbell Incline
Sets x Reps	68% x 8 73% x 6 76% x 5 80% x 4 88% x 2	68% x 8 73% x 6 76% x 5 80% x 4 88% x 2	68% x 8 73% x 6 76% x 5 80% x 4 88% x 2	68% x 8 73% x 6 76% x 5 80% x 4 88% x 2	68% x 8 73% x 6 76% x 5 80% x 4 88% x 2
AREA 2	**Platform**	**Platform**	**Platform**	**Platform**	**Platform**
Exercise	Heavy Barbell Shrugs	Heavy Barbell Shrugs	Heavy Barbell Shrugs	Heavy Barbell Shrugs	Heavy Barbell Shrugs
Sets x Reps	5 x 8	5 x 8	5 x 8	5 x 8	5 x 8
AREA 3A	**Dumbbell Racks**	**Dumbbell Racks**	**Dumbbell Racks**	**Dumbbell Racks**	**Dumbbell Racks**
Exercise	Barbell / Dumbbell Upright Rows	Barbell / Dumbbell Upright Rows	Barbell / Dumbbell Bicep Curls	Barbell / Dumbbell Bicep Curls	Barbell / Dumbbell Bicep Curls
Sets x Reps	2 x 8-10	2 x 8-10	2 x 8-10	2 x 8-10	2 x 8-10
AREA 3B	**Machine Area**	**Machine Area**	**Machine Area**	**Machine Area**	**Machine Area**
Exercise	Lat Pulls	Full Sit Ups	Triceps Pushdown	Straight Leg Raises or Wipers-Slight Bend	Neck Front Push
Sets x Reps	2 x 8-10	2 x 8-10	2 x 8-10	2 x 8-10	2 x 8-10

EXAMPLE: SUMMER STRENGTH & CONDITIONING: WEEKS 1 - 6					
WEEK 6 - TUESDAY					
NOTES	3 areas, 15 min rotation.				
	Group 1 Students	**Group 2 Students**	**Group 3 Students**	**Group 4 Students**	**Group 5 Students**
AREA 1	**Rack 1**	**Rack 2**	**Rack 3**	**Rack 4**	**Rack 5**
Exercise	Barbell Squat	Barbell Squat	Barbell Squat	Barbell Squat	Barbell Squat
Sets x Reps	63% x 8 68% x 6 73% x 5 75% x 5 78% x 5	63% x 8 68% x 6 73% x 5 75% x 5 78% x 5	63% x 8 68% x 6 73% x 5 75% x 5 78% x 5	63% x 8 68% x 6 73% x 5 75% x 5 78% x 5	63% x 8 68% x 6 73% x 5 75% x 5 78% x 5
AREA 2	**Platform**	**Platform**	**Platform**	**Platform**	**Platform**
Exercise	Heavy Barbell Deadlift	Heavy Barbell Deadlift	Heavy Barbell Deadlift	Heavy Barbell Deadlift	Heavy Barbell Deadlift
Sets x Reps	5 x 8	5 x 8	5 x 8	5 x 8	5 x 8
AREA 3A	**Dumbbell Racks**	**Dumbbell Racks**	**Dumbbell Racks**	**Dumbbell Racks**	**Dumbbell Racks**
Exercise	Barbell / Dumbbell Step Ups	Barbell / Dumbbell Step Ups	Barbell Lateral Lunge	Barbell Lateral Lunge	Barbell Lateral Lunge
Sets x Reps	2 x 8-10	2 x 8-10	2 x 8-10	2 x 8-10	2 x 8-10
AREA 3B	**Machine Area**	**Machine Area**	**Machine Area**	**Machine Area**	**Machine Area**
Exercise	Hamstring Curls	Leg Extensions	Front Planks	Front Plank Twist or Side Planks	Neck Back Push
Sets x Reps	2 x 8-10	2 x 8-10	2 x 8-10	2 x 8-10	2 x 8-10

EXAMPLE: SUMMER STRENGTH & CONDITIONING: WEEKS 1 - 6					
WEEK 6 - WEDNESDAY					
NOTES	3 areas, 15 min rotation.				
	Group 1 Students	**Group 2 Students**	**Group 3 Students**	**Group 4 Students**	**Group 5 Students**
AREA 1	**Rack 1**	**Rack 2**	**Rack 3**	**Rack 4**	**Rack 5**
Exercise	Barbell Incline	Barbell Incline	Barbell Incline	Close Grip Bench Press	Close Grip Bench Press
Sets x Reps	68% x 8 73% x 6 76% x 5 80% x 4 88% x 2	68% x 8 73% x 6 76% x 5 80% x 4 88% x 2	68% x 8 73% x 6 76% x 5 80% x 4 88% x 2	5 x 5 Add weight	5 x 5 Add weight
AREA 1	**Rack 6 (Smith Machine)**				
Exercise	Close Grip Bench Press				
Sets x Reps	5 x 5				
AREA 2	**Platform**	**Platform**	**Platform**	**Platform**	**Platform**
Exercise	Barbell Shrugs	Barbell Shrugs	Barbell Shrugs	Barbell Low Row	Barbell Low Row
Sets x Reps	5 x 8	5 x 8	5 x 8	5 x 8	5 x 8
AREA 3A	**Dumbbell Racks**	**Dumbbell Racks**	**Dumbbell Racks**	**Dumbbell Racks**	**Dumbbell Racks**
Exercise	Barbell / Dumbbell Upright Row	Barbell / Dumbbell Upright Row	Dumbbell Back Row	Dumbbell Back Row	Dumbbell Side Raise
Sets x Reps	2 x 8-10	2 x 8-10	2 x 8-10	2 x 8-10	2 x 8-10

AREA 3B	Machine Area	Dumbbell Racks	Dumbbell Racks		
Exercise	Dumbbell Side Raise	Dumbbell Rear Raise	Dumbbell Rear Raise		
Sets x Reps	2 x 8-10	2 x 8-10	2 x 8-10		
AREA 3C	Machine Area	Machine Area	Machine Area	Machine Area	
Exercise	Russian Twists	Triangle Crunch	Wide Leg Crunch	Neck RT Side	
Sets x Reps	2 x 10-25	2 x 10-25	2 x 10-25	2 x 8-10	

EXAMPLE: SUMMER STRENGTH & CONDITIONING: WEEKS 1 - 6					
WEEK 6 - THURSDAY					
NOTES	3 areas, 15 min rotation.				
	Group 1 Students	Group 2 Students	Group 3 Students	Group 4 Students	Group 5 Students
AREA 1	Rack 1	Rack 2	Rack 3	Rack 4	Rack 5
Exercise	Front Squat	Barbell Squat	Barbell Squat	Barbell Squat	Barbell Squat
Sets x Reps	63% x 8 68% x 8 73% x 6 73% x 5 73% x 5	63% x 8 68% x 8 73% x 6 73% x 5 73% x 5	63% x 8 68% x 8 73% x 6 73% x 5 73% x 5	63% x 8 68% x 8 73% x 6 73% x 5 73% x 5	63% x 8 68% x 8 73% x 6 73% x 5 73% x 5
AREA 2	Platform	Platform	Platform	Platform	Platform
Exercise	Heavy Barbell Deadlift	Heavy Barbell Deadlift	Heavy Barbell Deadlift	Heavy Barbell Deadlift	Heavy Barbell Deadlift
Sets x Reps	5 x 8	5 x 8	5 x 8	5 x 8	5 x 8
AREA 3A	Dumbbell Racks	Dumbbell Racks	Dumbbell Racks	Dumbbell Racks	Dumbbell Racks
Exercise	Barbell / Dumbbell Step Ups	Barbell / Dumbbell Step Ups	Barbell Lateral Lunge	Barbell Lateral Lunge	Barbell Lateral Lunge
Sets x Reps	2 x 10	2 x 10	2 x 10	2 x 10	2 x 10
AREA 3B	Machine Area	Machine Area	Machine Area	Machine Area	Machine Area
Exercise	Hamstring Curls	Leg Extensions	Front Planks	Front Plank Twists or Side Planks	Neck Back Push
Sets x Reps	2 x 10	2 x 10	2 x 10	2 x 10	2 x 10

1st DAY IN-SEASON: FIRST GAME IN 3 WEEKS: WEIGHTS 2x PER WEEK ONLY					
THURSDAY – LOWER BODY					
NOTES	3 areas, 15 min rotation.				
	Group 1 Students	Group 2 Students	Group 3 Students	Group 4 Students	Group 5 Students
AREA 1	Rack 1	Rack 2	Rack 3	Rack 4	Rack 5
Exercise	Barbell Squat	Barbell Squat	Barbell Squat	Barbell Squat	Barbell Squat
Sets x Reps	4 x 8-10	4 x 8-10	4 x 8-10	4 x 8-10	4 x 8-10
AREA 2	Platform	Platform	Platform	Platform	Platform
Exercise	Barbell Deadlift	Barbell Deadlift	Barbell Deadlift	Barbell Deadlift	Barbell Deadlift
Sets x Reps	4 x 8-10	4 x 8-10	4 x 8-10	4 x 8-10	4 x 8-10
AREA 3A	Dumbbell Racks	Dumbbell Racks	Dumbbell Racks	Dumbbell Racks	Dumbbell Racks
Exercise	Barbell / Dumbbell Step Ups	Barbell / Dumbbell Step Ups	Barbell Lat Lunge	Barbell Lat Lunge	Barbell Lat Lunge

Sets x Reps	2 x 8-10	2 x 8-10	2 x 8-10	2 x 8-10	2 x 8-10
AREA 3B	**Machine Area**	**Machine Area**	**Machine Area**	**Machine Area**	**Machine Area**
Exercise	Hamstring Curls	Leg Extensions	Front Planks	Front Plank Twist / Side Plank	Neck
Sets x Reps	2 x 8-10	2 x 8-10	2 x 8-10	2 x 8-10	2 x 8-10

MONDAY – UPPER BODY					
NOTES	3 areas, 15 min rotation.				
	Group 1 Students	**Group 2 Students**	**Group 3 Students**	**Group 4 Students**	**Group 5 Students**
AREA 1	**Rack 1**	**Rack 2**	**Rack 3**	**Rack 4**	**Rack 5**
Exercise	Barbell Incline	Barbell Incline	Barbell Incline	Barbell Incline	Barbell Incline
Sets x Reps	4 x 8-10	4 x 8-10	4 x 8-10	4 x 8-10	4 x 8-10
AREA 2	**Platform**	**Platform**	**Platform**	**Platform**	**Platform**
Exercise	Barbell Shrugs	Barbell Shrugs	Barbell Shrugs	Barbell Low Rows	Barbell Low Rows
Sets x Reps	4 x 8-10	4 x 8-10	4 x 8-10	4 x 8-10	4 x 8-10
AREA 3A	**Dumbbell Racks**	**Dumbbell Racks**	**Dumbbell Racks**	**Dumbbell Racks**	**Dumbbell Racks**
Exercise	Barbell / Dumbbell Upright Rows	Barbell / Dumbbell Upright Rows	Barbell / Dumbbell Bicep Curls	Barbell / Dumbbell Bicep Curls	Barbell / Dumbbell Bicep Curls
Sets x Reps	2 x 8-10	2 x 8-10	2 x 8-10	2 x 8-10	2 x 8-10
AREA 3B	**Machine Area**	**Machine Area**	**Machine Area**	**Machine Area**	**Machine Area**
Exercise	Lat Pulls	Full Sit Ups	Triceps Pushdowns	Straight Leg Raises or Windshield Wipers	Neck Push
Sets x Reps	2 x 8-10	2 x 8-10	2 x 8-10	2 x 8-10	2 x 8-10

THURSDAY – LOWER BODY					
NOTES	3 areas, 15 min rotation.				
	Group 1 Students	**Group 2 Students**	**Group 3 Students**	**Group 4 Students**	**Group 5 Students**
AREA 1	**Rack 1**	**Rack 2**	**Rack 3**	**Rack 4**	**Rack 5**
Exercise	Front Squat	Front Squat	Front Squat	Front Squat	Front Squat
Sets x Reps	63% x 8 68% x 8 68% x 8 73% x 6 73% x 6	63% x 8 68% x 8 68% x 8 73% x 6 73% x 6	63% x 8 68% x 8 68% x 8 73% x 6 73% x 6	63% x 8 68% x 8 68% x 8 73% x 6 73% x 6	63% x 8 68% x 8 68% x 8 73% x 6 73% x 6
AREA 2	**Platform**	**Platform**	**Platform**	**Platform**	**Platform**
Exercise	Barbell Russian Deadlift	Barbell Russian Deadlift	Barbell Russian Deadlift	Barbell Russian Deadlift	Barbell Russian Deadlift
Sets x Reps	73% x 8 73% x 8 73% x 8 78% x 6 78% x 6	73% x 8 73% x 8 73% x 8 78% x 6 78% x 6	73% x 8 73% x 8 73% x 8 78% x 6 78% x 6	73% x 8 73% x 8 73% x 8 78% x 6 78% x 6	73% x 8 73% x 8 73% x 8 78% x 6 78% x 6
AREA 3A	**Dumbbell Racks**	**Dumbbell Racks**	**Dumbbell Racks**	**Dumbbell Racks**	**Dumbbell Racks**
Exercise	4-way Dumbbell Lunge	4-way Dumbbell Lunge	Barbell Lateral Lunge	Barbell Lateral Lunge	Barbell Lateral Lunge

Sets x Reps	2 x 8-10	2 x 8-10	2 x 8-10	2 x 8-10	2 x 8-10
AREA 3B	**Machine Area**	**Machine Area**	**Machine Area**	**Machine Area**	**Machine Area**
Exercise	Hamstring Curls	Single Leg Press	Bicycles	V-Ups or Side Planks	Side Crunch
Sets x Reps	2 x 8-10	2 x 8-10	2 x 8-10	2 x 8-10	2 x 8-10
AREA 3C	**Outside**	**Machine Area**			
Exercise	Walking Lunge	Neck LF Side			
Sets x Reps	2 x 8-10	2 x 8-10			

MONDAY – UPPER BODY					
NOTES	3 areas, 15 min rotation.				
	Group 1 Students	**Group 2 Students**	**Group 3 Students**	**Group 4 Students**	**Group 5 Students**
AREA 1	**Rack 1**	**Rack 2**	**Rack 3**	**Rack 4**	**Rack 5**
Exercise	Barbell Incline	Barbell Incline	Barbell Incline	Close Grip Bench Press	Close Grip Bench Press
Sets x Reps	63% x 8 70% x 8 70% x 8 73% x 6 73% x 6	63% x 8 70% x 8 70% x 8 73% x 6 73% x 6	63% x 8 70% x 8 70% x 8 73% x 6 73% x 6	5 x 6-8	5 x 6-8
AREA 1	**Rack 6 Smith Machine**				
Exercise	Close Grip Bench Press				
Sets x Reps	5 x 6-8				
AREA 2	**Platform**	**Platform**	**Platform**	**Platform**	**Platform**
Exercise	Barbell Heavy Shrugs	Barbell Heavy Shrugs	Barbell Heavy Shrugs	Barbell Heavy Shrugs	Barbell Heavy Shrugs
Sets x Reps	5 x 8	5 x 8	5 x 8	5 x 8	5 x 8
AREA 3A	**Dumbbell Racks**	**Dumbbell Racks**	**Dumbbell Racks**	**Dumbbell Racks**	**Dumbbell Racks**
Exercise	Barbell / Dumbbell Upright Rows	Barbell / Dumbbell Upright Rows	Dumbbell Back Rows	Dumbbell Back Rows	Dumbbell Side Raise
Sets x Reps	2 x 8-10	2 x 8-10	2 x 8-10	2 x 8-10	2 x 8-10
AREA 3B	**Machine Area**	**Dumbbell Racks**	**Dumbbell Racks**		
Exercise	Dumbbell Side Raise	Dumbbell Rear Raise	Dumbbell Rear Raise		
Sets x Reps	2 x 8-10	2 x 8-10	2 x 8-10		
AREA 3C	**Machine Area**	**Machine Area**	**Machine Area**	**Machine Area**	
Sets x Reps	2 x 8-10	2 x 8-10	2 x 8-10	2 x 8-10	

THURSDAY – LOWER BODY					
NOTES	3 areas, 15 min rotation.				
	Group 1 Students	**Group 2 Students**	**Group 3 Students**	**Group 4 Students**	**Group 5 Students**
AREA 1	**Rack 1**	**Rack 2**	**Rack 3**	**Rack 4**	**Rack 5**
Exercise	Barbell Squat	Barbell Squat	Barbell Squat	Barbell Squat	Barbell Squat
Sets x Reps	63% x 8	63% x 8	63% x 8	63% x 8	63% x 8

	68% x 8	68% x 8	68% x 8	68% x 8	68% x 8
	68% x 8	68% x 8	68% x 8	68% x 8	68% x 8
	73% x 6	73% x 6	73% x 6	73% x 6	73% x 6
	73% x 6	73% x 6	73% x 6	73% x 6	73% x 6
AREA 2	**Platform**	**Platform**	**Platform**	**Platform**	**Platform**
Exercise	Barbell Deadlift	Barbell Deadlift	Barbell Deadlift	Barbell Deadlift	Barbell Deadlift
Sets x Reps	73% x 8	73% x 8	73% x 8	73% x 8	73% x 8
	73% x 8	73% x 8	73% x 8	73% x 8	73% x 8
	73% x 8	73% x 8	73% x 8	73% x 8	73% x 8
	78% x 6	78% x 6	78% x 6	78% x 6	78% x 6
	78% x 6	78% x 6	78% x 6	78% x 6	78% x 6
AREA 3A	**Dumbbell Racks**	**Dumbbell Racks**	**Dumbbell Racks**	**Dumbbell Racks**	**Dumbbell Racks**
Exercise	4-way Dumbbell Lunge	4-way Dumbbell Lunge	Barbell Lateral Lunge	Barbell Lateral Lunge	Barbell Lateral Lunge
Sets x Reps	2 x 8-10	2 x 8-10	2 x 8-10	2 x 8-10	2 x 8-10
AREA 3B	**Machine Area**	**Machine Area**	**Machine Area**	**Machine Area**	**Machine Area**
Exercise	Hamstring Curls	Single Leg Press	Bicycles	V-Ups or Side Planks	Side Crunch
Sets x Reps	2 x 8-10	2 x 8-10	2 x 8-10	2 x 8-10	2 x 8-10
AREA 3C	**Outside**	**Machine Area**			
Exercise	Walking Lunge	Neck LF Side			
Sets x Reps	2 x 8-10	2 x 8-10			

IN-SEASON: GAME WEEKS					
MONDAY - LOWER BODY PERFORMED 4-5 DAYS BEFORE GAME DAY					
	Group 1 Students	**Group 2 Students**	**Group 3 Students**	**Group 4 Students**	**Group 5 Students**
AREA 1	**Rack 1**	**Rack 2**	**Rack 3**	**Rack 4**	**Rack 5**
Exercise	Barbell Squat	Barbell Squat	Barbell Squat	Barbell Squat	Barbell Squat
Sets x Reps	60% x 10	60% x 10	60% x 10	60% x 10	60% x 10
	73% x 5	73% x 5	73% x 5	73% x 5	73% x 5
	73% x 5	73% x 5	73% x 5	73% x 5	73% x 5
	75% x 5	75% x 5	75% x 5	75% x 5	75% x 5
	75% x 5	75% x 5	75% x 5	75% x 5	75% x 5
AREA 2	**Platform**	**Platform**	**Platform**	**Platform**	**Platform**
Exercise	Heavy Barbell Deadlift	Heavy Barbell Deadlift	Heavy Barbell Deadlift	Heavy Barbell Deadlift	Heavy Barbell Deadlift
Sets x Reps	73% x 5	73% x 5	73% x 5	73% x 5	73% x 5
	73% x 5	73% x 5	73% x 5	73% x 5	73% x 5
	73% x 5	73% x 5	73% x 5	73% x 5	73% x 5
	78% x 5	78% x 5	78% x 5	78% x 5	78% x 5
	73% x 5	73% x 5	73% x 5	73% x 5	73% x 5
AREA 3A	**Dumbbell Racks**	**Dumbbell Racks**	**Dumbbell Racks**	**Dumbbell Racks**	**Dumbbell Racks**
Exercise	Barbell / Dumbbell Step Ups	Barbell / Dumbbell Step Ups	Barbell Lateral Lunge	Barbell Lateral Lunge	Barbell Lateral Lunge
Sets x Reps	2 x 8-10	2 x 8-10	2 x 8-10	2 x 8-10	2 x 8-10
AREA 3B	**Machine Area**	**Machine Area**	**Machine Area**	**Machine Area**	**Machine Area**
Exercise	Hamstring Curls	Leg Extensions	Front Planks	Front Plank Twist / Side Plank	Neck
Sets x Reps	2 x 8-10	2 x 8-10	2 x 8-10	2 x 8-10	2 x 8-10

IN-SEASON: GAME WEEKS				
WEDNESDAY - UPPER BODY				
	Group 1 Students	Group 2 Students	Group 3 Students	Group 4 Students	Group 5 Students
---	---	---	---	---	---
AREA 1	**Rack 1**	**Rack 2**	**Rack 3**	**Rack 4**	**Rack 5**
Exercise	Barbell Incline	Barbell Incline	Barbell Incline	Close-grip Bench Press	Close-grip Bench Press
Sets x Reps	60% x 10 70% x 5 73% x 5 75% x 5 75% x 5	60% x 10 70% x 5 73% x 5 75% x 5 75% x 5	60% x 10 70% x 5 73% x 5 75% x 5 75% x 5	5 x 5	5 x 5
AREA 1	**Rack 6 (Smith Machine)**				
Exercise	Close-grip Bench Press				
Sets x Reps	5 x 5				
AREA 2	**Platform**	**Platform**	**Platform**	**Platform**	**Platform**
Exercise	Heavy Barbell Shrugs	Heavy Barbell Shrugs	Heavy Barbell Shrugs	Heavy Barbell Shrugs	Heavy Barbell Shrugs
Sets x Reps	5 x 6	5 x 6	5 x 6	5 x 6	5 x 6
AREA 3A	**Dumbbell Racks**	**Dumbbell Racks**	**Dumbbell Racks**	**Dumbbell Racks**	**Dumbbell Racks**
Exercise	Barbell / Dumbbell Step Ups	Barbell / Dumbbell Step Ups	Dumbbell Back Rows	Dumbbell Back Rows	Dumbbell Side Raise
Sets x Reps	2 x 8-10	2 x 8-10	2 x 8-10	2 x 8-10	2 x 8-10
AREA 3B	**Machine Area**	**Dumbbell Racks**	**Dumbbell Racks**		
Exercise	Dumbbell Side Raise	Dumbbell Rear Raise	Dumbbell Rear Raise		
Sets x Reps	2 x 8-10	2 x 8-10	2 x 8-10		
AREA 3B	**Machine Area**	**Machine Area**	**Machine Area**	**Machine Area**	
Exercise	Russian Twist	Crunch	Wide Leg Crunch	Neck RT Side	
Sets x Reps	2 x 8-10	2 x 8-10	2 x 8-10	2 x 8-10	

IN-SEASON: GAME WEEKS				
MONDAY - LOWER BODY				
	Group 1 Students	Group 2 Students	Group 3 Students	Group 4 Students	Group 5 Students
---	---	---	---	---	---
AREA 1	**Rack 1**	**Rack 2**	**Rack 3**	**Rack 4**	**Rack 5**
Exercise	Barbell Squat	Barbell Squat	Barbell Squat	Barbell Squat	Barbell Squat
Sets x Reps	60% x 10 73% x 5 76% x 5 79% x 5 83% x 4	60% x 10 73% x 5 76% x 5 79% x 5 83% x 4	60% x 10 73% x 5 76% x 5 79% x 5 83% x 4	60% x 10 73% x 5 76% x 5 79% x 5 83% x 4	60% x 10 73% x 5 76% x 5 79% x 5 83% x 4
AREA 2	**Platform**	**Platform**	**Platform**	**Platform**	**Platform**
Exercise	Heavy Barbell Deadlift	Heavy Barbell Deadlift	Heavy Barbell Deadlift	Heavy Barbell Deadlift	Heavy Barbell Deadlift
Sets x Reps	73% x 5 73% x 5 73% x 5 78% x 5	73% x 5 73% x 5 73% x 5 78% x 5	73% x 5 73% x 5 73% x 5 78% x 5	73% x 5 73% x 5 73% x 5 78% x 5	73% x 5 73% x 5 73% x 5 78% x 5

	78% x 5	78% x 5	78% x 5	78% x 5	78% x 5
AREA 3A	**Dumbbell Racks**	**Dumbbell Racks**	**Dumbbell Racks**	**Dumbbell Racks**	**Dumbbell Racks**
Exercise	Barbell / Dumbbell Step Ups	Barbell / Dumbbell Step Ups	Barbell Lateral Lunge	Barbell Lateral Lunge	Barbell Lateral Lunge
Sets x Reps	2 x 8-10	2 x 8-10	2 x 8-10	2 x 8-10	2 x 8-10
AREA 3B	**Machine Area**	**Dumbbell Racks**	**Dumbbell Racks**	**Dumbbell Racks**	**Dumbbell Racks**
Exercise	Hamstring Curls	Leg Extensions	Front Planks	Front Plank Twist	Neck Back Push
Sets x Reps	2 x 8-10	2 x 8-10	2 x 8-10	2 x 8-10	2 x 8-10

IN-SEASON: GAME WEEKS					
WEDNESDAY - UPPER BODY					
	Group 1 Students	**Group 2 Students**	**Group 3 Students**	**Group 4 Students**	**Group 5 Students**
AREA 1	**Rack 1**	**Rack 2**	**Rack 3**	**Rack 4**	**Rack 5**
Exercise	Barbell Incline	Barbell Incline	Barbell Incline	Close-grip Bench Press	Close-grip Bench Press
Sets x Reps	60% x 10 73% x 5 76% x 5 79% x 5 83% x 4	60% x 10 73% x 5 76% x 5 79% x 5 83% x 4	60% x 10 73% x 5 76% x 5 79% x 5 83% x 4	5 x 5	5 x 5
AREA 1	**Rack 6 (Smith Machine)**				
Exercise	Close-grip Bench Press				
Sets x Reps	5 x 5				
AREA 2	**Platform**	**Platform**	**Platform**	**Platform**	**Platform**
Exercise	Heavy Barbell Shrugs	Heavy Barbell Shrugs	Heavy Barbell Shrugs	Heavy Barbell Shrugs	Heavy Barbell Shrugs
Sets x Reps	5 x 6	5 x 6	5 x 6	5 x 6	5 x 6
AREA 3A	**Dumbbell Racks**	**Dumbbell Racks**	**Dumbbell Racks**	**Dumbbell Racks**	**Dumbbell Racks**
Exercise	Barbell / Dumbbell Upright Rows	Barbell / Dumbbell Upright Rows	Dumbbell Back Rows	Dumbbell Back Rows	Dumbbell Side Raise
Sets x Reps	2 x 8-10	2 x 8-10	2 x 8-10	2 x 8-10	2 x 8-10
AREA 3B	**Machine Area**	**Dumbbell Racks**	**Dumbbell Racks**		
Exercise	Dumbbell Side Raise	Dumbbell Rear Raise	Dumbbell Rear Raise		
Sets x Reps	2 x 8-10	2 x 8-10	2 x 8-10		
AREA 3B	**Machine Area**	**Machine Area**	**Machine Area**	**Machine Area**	
Exercise	Russian Twist	Crunch	Wide Leg Crunch	Neck RT Side	
Sets x Reps	2 x 8-10	2 x 8-10	2 x 8-10	2 x 8-10	

IN-SEASON: GAME WEEKS					
MONDAY - LOWER BODY					
	Group 1 Students	**Group 2 Students**	**Group 3 Students**	**Group 4 Students**	**Group 5 Students**
AREA 1	**Rack 1**	**Rack 2**	**Rack 3**	**Rack 4**	**Rack 5**
Exercise	Barbell Squat	Barbell Squat	Barbell Squat	Barbell Squat	Barbell Squat

Sets x Reps	60% x 10 75% x 5 75% x 5 75% x 5 75% x 5	60% x 10 75% x 5 75% x 5 75% x 5 75% x 5	60% x 10 75% x 5 75% x 5 75% x 5 75% x 5	60% x 10 75% x 5 75% x 5 75% x 5 75% x 5	60% x 10 75% x 5 75% x 5 75% x 5 75% x 5
AREA 2	**Platform**	**Platform**	**Platform**	**Platform**	**Platform**
Exercise	Romanian Deadlifts	Romanian Deadlifts	Romanian Deadlifts	Romanian Deadlifts	Romanian Deadlifts
Sets x Reps	70% x 5 70% x 5 73% x 5 75% x 5 75% x 5	70% x 5 70% x 5 73% x 5 75% x 5 75% x 5	70% x 5 70% x 5 73% x 5 75% x 5 75% x 5	70% x 5 70% x 5 73% x 5 75% x 5 75% x 5	70% x 5 70% x 5 73% x 5 75% x 5 75% x 5
AREA 3A	**Dumbbell Racks**	**Dumbbell Racks**	**Dumbbell Racks**	**Dumbbell Racks**	**Dumbbell Racks**
Exercise	Barbell / Dumbbell Step Ups	Barbell / Dumbbell Step Ups	Barbell Lateral Lunge	Barbell Lateral Lunge	Barbell Lateral Lunge
Sets x Reps	2 x 8-10	2 x 8-10	2 x 8-10	2 x 8-10	2 x 8-10
AREA 3B	**Machine Area**	**Machine Area**	**Machine Area**	**Machine Area**	**Machine Area**
Exercise	Hamstring Curls	Leg Extensions	Front Planks	Front Plank Twist	Neck Back Push
Sets x Reps	2 x 8-10	2 x 8-10	2 x 8-10	2 x 8-10	2 x 8-10

IN-SEASON: GAME WEEKS					
WEDNESDAY - UPPER BODY					
	Group 1 Students	Group 2 Students	Group 3 Students	Group 4 Students	Group 5 Students
AREA 1	**Rack 1**	**Rack 2**	**Rack 3**	**Rack 4**	**Rack 5**
Exercise	Barbell Incline	Barbell Incline	Barbell Incline	Close-grip Bench Press	Close-grip Bench Press
Sets x Reps	60% x 10 70% x 5 73% x 5 75% x 5 75% x 5	60% x 10 70% x 5 73% x 5 75% x 5 75% x 5	60% x 10 70% x 5 73% x 5 75% x 5 75% x 5	5 x 5	5 x 5
AREA 1	**Rack 6 (Smith Machine)**				
Exercise	Close-grip Bench Press				
Sets x Reps	5 x 5				
AREA 2	**Platform**	**Platform**	**Platform**	**Platform**	**Platform**
Exercise	Heavy Barbell Shrugs	Heavy Barbell Shrugs	Heavy Barbell Shrugs	Heavy Barbell Shrugs	Heavy Barbell Shrugs
Sets x Reps	5 x 5	5 x 5	5 x 5	5 x 5	5 x 5
AREA 3A	**Dumbbell Racks**	**Dumbbell Racks**	**Dumbbell Racks**	**Dumbbell Racks**	**Dumbbell Racks**
Exercise	Barbell / Dumbbell Upright Rows	Barbell / Dumbbell Upright Rows	Dumbbell Back Rows	Dumbbell Back Rows	Dumbbell Side Raise
Sets x Reps	2 x 8-10	2 x 8-10	2 x 8-10	2 x 8-10	2 x 8-10
AREA 3B	**Machine Area**	**Dumbbell Racks**	**Dumbbell Racks**		
Exercise	Dumbbell Side Raise	Dumbbell Rear Raise	Dumbbell Rear Raise		
Sets x Reps	2 x 8-10	2 x 8-10	2 x 8-10		

AREA 3B	Machine Area	Machine Area	Machine Area	Machine Area	
Exercise	Russian Twist	Triangle Crunch	Wide Leg Crunch	Neck RT Side	
Sets x Reps	2 x 8-10	2 x 8-10	2 x 8-10	2 x 8-10	

IN-SEASON: GAME WEEKS					
MONDAY - LOWER BODY					
	Group 1 Students	Group 2 Students	Group 3 Students	Group 4 Students	Group 5 Students
AREA 1	Rack 1	Rack 2	Rack 3	Rack 4	Rack 5
Exercise	Barbell Squat	Barbell Squat	Barbell Squat	Barbell Squat	Barbell Squat
Sets x Reps	60% x 10 73% x 5 76% x 5 79% x 5 83% x 4	60% x 10 73% x 5 76% x 5 79% x 5 83% x 4	60% x 10 73% x 5 76% x 5 79% x 5 83% x 4	60% x 10 73% x 5 76% x 5 79% x 5 83% x 4	60% x 10 73% x 5 76% x 5 79% x 5 83% x 4
AREA 2	Platform	Platform	Platform	Platform	Platform
Exercise	Romanian Deadlifts	Romanian Deadlifts	Romanian Deadlifts	Romanian Deadlifts	Romanian Deadlifts
Sets x Reps	73% x 5 73% x 5 73% x 5 75% x 5 75% x 5	73% x 5 73% x 5 73% x 5 75% x 5 75% x 5	73% x 5 73% x 5 73% x 5 75% x 5 75% x 5	73% x 5 73% x 5 73% x 5 75% x 5 75% x 5	73% x 5 73% x 5 73% x 5 75% x 5 75% x 5
AREA 3A	Dumbbell Racks	Dumbbell Racks	Dumbbell Racks	Dumbbell Racks	Dumbbell Racks
Exercise	Barbell / Dumbbell Step Ups	Barbell / Dumbbell Step Ups	Barbell Lateral Lunge	Barbell Lateral Lunge	Barbell Lateral Lunge
Sets x Reps	2 x 8-10	2 x 8-10	2 x 8-10	2 x 8-10	2 x 8-10
AREA 3B	Machine Area	Machine Area	Machine Area	Machine Area	Machine Area
Exercise	Hamstring Curls	Leg Extensions	Front Planks	Front Plank Twist	Neck Back Push
Sets x Reps	2 x 8-10	2 x 8-10	2 x 8-10	2 x 8-10	2 x 8-10

IN-SEASON: GAME WEEKS					
WEDNESDAY - UPPER BODY					
	Group 1 Students	Group 2 Students	Group 3 Students	Group 4 Students	Group 5 Students
AREA 1	Rack 1	Rack 2	Rack 3	Rack 4	Rack 5
Exercise	Barbell Incline	Barbell Incline	Barbell Incline	Close-grip Bench Press	Close-grip Bench Press
Sets x Reps	60% x 10 73% x 5 79% x 5 83% x 4 85% x 3	60% x 10 73% x 5 79% x 5 83% x 4 85% x 3	60% x 10 73% x 5 79% x 5 83% x 4 85% x 3	5 x 5	5 x 5
AREA 1	Rack 6 (Smith Machine)				
Exercise	Close-grip Bench Press				
Sets x Reps	5 x 5				
AREA 2	Platform	Platform	Platform	Platform	Platform
Exercise	Heavy Barbell Shrugs	Heavy Barbell Shrugs	Heavy Barbell Shrugs	Heavy Barbell Shrugs	Heavy Barbell Shrugs

Sets x Reps	5 x 5	5 x 5	5 x 5	5 x 5	5 x 5
AREA 3A	**Dumbbell Racks**	**Dumbbell Racks**	**Dumbbell Racks**	**Dumbbell Racks**	**Dumbbell Racks**
Exercise	Barbell / Dumbbell Upright Rows	Barbell / Dumbbell Upright Rows	Dumbbell Back Rows	Dumbbell Back Rows	Dumbbell Side Raise
Sets x Reps	2 x 8-10	2 x 8-10	2 x 8-10	2 x 8-10	2 x 8-10
AREA 3B	**Machine Area**	**Dumbbell Racks**	**Dumbbell Racks**		
Exercise	Dumbbell Side Raise	Dumbbell Rear Raise	Dumbbell Rear Raise		
Sets x Reps	2 x 8-10	2 x 8-10	2 x 8-10		
AREA 3B	**Machine Area**	**Machine Area**	**Machine Area**	**Machine Area**	
Exercise	Russian Twist	Triangle Crunch	Wide Leg Crunch	Neck RT Side	
Sets x Reps	2 x 8-10	2 x 8-10	2 x 8-10	2 x 8-10	

IN-SEASON: GAME WEEKS					
MONDAY - LOWER BODY (ADD ROLLER)					
	Group 1 Students	**Group 2 Students**	**Group 3 Students**	**Group 4 Students**	**Group 5 Students**
AREA 1	**Rack 1**	**Rack 2**	**Rack 3**	**Rack 4**	**Rack 5**
Exercise	Barbell Squat	Barbell Squat	Barbell Squat	Barbell Squat	Barbell Squat
Sets x Reps	60% x 10 65% x 8 70% x 8 73% x 6	60% x 10 65% x 8 70% x 8 73% x 6	60% x 10 65% x 8 70% x 8 73% x 6	60% x 10 65% x 8 70% x 8 73% x 6	60% x 10 65% x 8 70% x 8 73% x 6
AREA 2	**Platform**	**Platform**	**Platform**	**Platform**	**Platform**
Exercise	Romanian Deadlifts	Romanian Deadlifts	Romanian Deadlifts	Romanian Deadlifts	Romanian Deadlifts
Sets x Reps	73% x 5 73% x 5 73% x 5 73% x 5 73% x 5	73% x 5 73% x 5 73% x 5 73% x 5 73% x 5	73% x 5 73% x 5 73% x 5 73% x 5 73% x 5	73% x 5 73% x 5 73% x 5 73% x 5 73% x 5	73% x 5 73% x 5 73% x 5 73% x 5 73% x 5
AREA 3A	**Dumbbell Racks**	**Dumbbell Racks**	**Dumbbell Racks**	**Dumbbell Racks**	**Dumbbell Racks**
Exercise	Barbell / Dumbbell Step Ups	Barbell / Dumbbell Step Ups	Barbell Lateral Lunge	Barbell Lateral Lunge	Barbell Lateral Lunge
Sets x Reps	2 x 8-10	2 x 8-10	2 x 8-10	2 x 8-10	2 x 8-10
AREA 3B	**Machine Area**	**Machine Area**	**Machine Area**	**Machine Area**	**Machine Area**
Exercise	Hamstring Curls	Leg Extensions	Roller Stretch	Front Plank Twist	Neck Back Push
Sets x Reps	2 x 8-10	2 x 8-10	2 x 8-10	2 x 8-10	2 x 8-10

IN-SEASON: GAME WEEKS					
WEDNESDAY - UPPER BODY (ADD ROLLER)					
	Group 1 Students	**Group 2 Students**	**Group 3 Students**	**Group 4 Students**	**Group 5 Students**
AREA 1	**Rack 1**	**Rack 2**	**Rack 3**	**Rack 4**	**Rack 5**
Exercise	Barbell Incline	Barbell Incline	Barbell Incline	Close-grip Bench Press	Close-grip Bench Press
Sets x Reps	60% x 10 70% x 5 73% x 5	60% x 10 70% x 5 73% x 5	60% x 10 70% x 5 73% x 5	5 x 5	5 x 5

	75% x 5 75% x 5	75% x 5 75% x 5	75% x 5 75% x 5		
AREA 1	**Rack 6 (Smith Machine)**				
Exercise	Close-grip Bench Press				
Sets x Reps	5 x 5				
AREA 2	**Platform**	**Platform**	**Platform**	**Platform**	**Platform**
Exercise	Heavy Barbell Shrugs	Heavy Barbell Shrugs	Heavy Barbell Shrugs	Heavy Barbell Shrugs	Heavy Barbell Shrugs
Sets x Reps	5 x 5	5 x 5	5 x 5	5 x 5	5 x 5
AREA 3A	**Dumbbell Racks**	**Dumbbell Racks**	**Dumbbell Racks**	**Dumbbell Racks**	**Dumbbell Racks**
Exercise	Barbell / Dumbbell Upright Rows	Barbell / Dumbbell Upright Rows	Dumbbell Back Rows	Dumbbell Back Rows	Dumbbell Side Raise
Sets x Reps	2 x 8-10	2 x 8-10	2 x 8-10	2 x 8-10	2 x 8-10
AREA 3B	**Machine Area**	**Dumbbell Racks**	**Dumbbell Racks**		
Exercise	Dumbbell Side Raise	Dumbbell Rear Raise	Dumbbell Rear Raise		
Sets x Reps	2 x 8-10	2 x 8-10	2 x 8-10		
AREA 3B	**Machine Area**	**Machine Area**	**Machine Area**	**Machine Area**	
Exercise	Russian Twist	Triangle Crunch	Wide Leg Crunch	Neck RT Side	
Sets x Reps	2 x 8-10	2 x 8-10	2 x 8-10	2 x 8-10	

IN-SEASON: GAME WEEKS					
MONDAY - LOWER BODY (ADD ROLLER)					
	Group 1 Students	**Group 2 Students**	**Group 3 Students**	**Group 4 Students**	**Group 5 Students**
AREA 1	**Rack 1**	**Rack 2**	**Rack 3**	**Rack 4**	**Rack 5**
Exercise	Barbell Squat	Barbell Squat	Barbell Squat	Barbell Squat	Barbell Squat
Sets x Reps	60% x 10 65% x 8 70% x 8 70% x 8	60% x 10 65% x 8 70% x 8 70% x 8	60% x 10 65% x 8 70% x 8 70% x 8	60% x 10 65% x 8 70% x 8 70% x 8	60% x 10 65% x 8 70% x 8 70% x 8
AREA 2	**Platform**	**Platform**	**Platform**	**Platform**	**Platform**
Exercise	Romanian Deadlifts	Romanian Deadlifts	Romanian Deadlifts	Romanian Deadlifts	Romanian Deadlifts
Sets x Reps	70% x 8 70% x 8 73% x 6 73% x 6 73% x 6	70% x 8 70% x 8 73% x 6 73% x 6 73% x 6	70% x 8 70% x 8 73% x 6 73% x 6 73% x 6	70% x 8 70% x 8 73% x 6 73% x 6 73% x 6	70% x 8 70% x 8 73% x 6 73% x 6 73% x 6
AREA 3A	**Dumbbell Racks**	**Dumbbell Racks**	**Dumbbell Racks**	**Dumbbell Racks**	**Dumbbell Racks**
Exercise	Barbell / Dumbbell Step Ups	Barbell / Dumbbell Step Ups	Barbell Lateral Lunge	Barbell Lateral Lunge	Barbell Lateral Lunge
Sets x Reps	2 x 8-10	2 x 8-10	2 x 8-10	2 x 8-10	2 x 8-10
AREA 3B	**Machine Area**	**Machine Area**	**Machine Area**	**Machine Area**	**Machine Area**
Exercise	Hamstring Curls	Leg Extensions	Roller Stretch	Front Plank Twist	Neck Back Push
Sets x Reps	2 x 8-10	2 x 8-10	2 x 8-10	2 x 8-10	2 x 8-10

IN-SEASON: GAME WEEKS					
WEDNESDAY - UPPER BODY (ADD ROLLER)					
	Group 1 Students	**Group 2 Students**	**Group 3 Students**	**Group 4 Students**	**Group 5 Students**
AREA 1	**Rack 1**	**Rack 2**	**Rack 3**	**Rack 4**	**Rack 5**
Exercise	Barbell Incline	Barbell Incline	Barbell Incline	Close-grip Bench Press	Close-grip Bench Press
Sets x Reps	60% x 10 65% x 8 70% x 8 73% x 6	60% x 10 65% x 8 70% x 8 73% x 6	60% x 10 65% x 8 70% x 8 73% x 6	4 x 6	4 x 6
AREA 1	**Rack 6 (Smith Machine)**				
Exercise	Close-grip Bench Press				
Sets x Reps	4 x 6				
AREA 2	**Platform**	**Platform**	**Platform**	**Platform**	**Platform**
Exercise	Heavy Barbell Shrugs	Heavy Barbell Shrugs	Heavy Barbell Shrugs	Heavy Barbell Shrugs	Heavy Barbell Shrugs
Sets x Reps	4 x 6	4 x 6	4 x 6	4 x 6	4 x 6
AREA 3A	**Dumbbell Racks**	**Dumbbell Racks**	**Dumbbell Racks**	**Dumbbell Racks**	**Dumbbell Racks**
Exercise	Barbell / Dumbbell Upright Rows	Barbell / Dumbbell Upright Rows	Dumbbell Back Rows	Dumbbell Back Rows	Dumbbell Side Raise
Sets x Reps	2 x 8-10	2 x 8-10	2 x 8-10	2 x 8-10	2 x 8-10
AREA 3B	**Machine Area**	**Dumbbell Racks**	**Dumbbell Racks**		
Exercise	Dumbbell Side Raise	Dumbbell Rear Raise	Dumbbell Rear Raise		
Sets x Reps	2 x 8-10	2 x 8-10	2 x 8-10		
AREA 3B	**Machine Area**	**Machine Area**	**Machine Area**	**Machine Area**	
Exercise	Russian Twist	Triangle Crunch	Roller Stretch	Neck RT Side	
Sets x Reps	2 x 8-10	2 x 8-10	2 x 8-10	2 x 8-10	

IN-SEASON: GAME WEEKS					
MONDAY - LOWER BODY (ADD ROLLER)					
	Group 1 Students	**Group 2 Students**	**Group 3 Students**	**Group 4 Students**	**Group 5 Students**
AREA 1	**Rack 1**	**Rack 2**	**Rack 3**	**Rack 4**	**Rack 5**
Exercise	Barbell Squat	Barbell Squat	Barbell Squat	Barbell Squat	Barbell Squat
Sets x Reps	60% x 10 63% x 10 67% x 8 67% x 8	60% x 10 63% x 10 67% x 8 67% x 8	60% x 10 63% x 10 67% x 8 67% x 8	60% x 10 63% x 10 67% x 8 67% x 8	60% x 10 63% x 10 67% x 8 67% x 8
AREA 2	**Platform**	**Platform**	**Platform**	**Platform**	**Platform**
Exercise	Romanian Deadlifts	Romanian Deadlifts	Romanian Deadlifts	Romanian Deadlifts	Romanian Deadlifts
Sets x Reps	65% x 10 68% x 10 73% x 8 73% x 8	65% x 10 68% x 10 73% x 8 73% x 8	65% x 10 68% x 10 73% x 8 73% x 8	65% x 10 68% x 10 73% x 8 73% x 8	65% x 10 68% x 10 73% x 8 73% x 8

AREA 3A	Dumbbell Racks	Dumbbell Racks	Dumbbell Racks	Dumbbell Racks	Dumbbell Racks
Exercise	Barbell / Dumbbell Step Ups	Barbell / Dumbbell Step Ups	Barbell Lateral Lunge	Barbell Lateral Lunge	Barbell Lateral Lunge
Sets x Reps	2 x 8-10	2 x 8-10	2 x 8-10	2 x 8-10	2 x 8-10
AREA 3B	Machine Area	Machine Area	Machine Area	Machine Area	Machine Area
Exercise	Hamstring Curls	Leg Extensions	Roller Stretch	Front Plank Twist	Neck Back Push
Sets x Reps	2 x 8-10	2 x 8-10	2 x 8-10	2 x 8-10	2 x 8-10

IN-SEASON: GAME WEEKS					
WEDNESDAY - UPPER BODY (ADD ROLLER)					
	Group 1 Students	Group 2 Students	Group 3 Students	Group 4 Students	Group 5 Students
AREA 1	Rack 1	Rack 2	Rack 3	Rack 4	Rack 5
Exercise	Barbell Incline	Barbell Incline	Barbell Incline	Close-grip Bench Press	Close-grip Bench Press
Sets x Reps	60% x 10 65% x 8 70% x 8 70% x 8	60% x 10 65% x 8 70% x 8 70% x 8	60% x 10 65% x 8 70% x 8 70% x 8	4 x 8	4 x 8
AREA 1	Rack 6 (Smith Machine)				
Exercise	Close-grip Bench Press				
Sets x Reps	4 x 8				
AREA 2	Platform	Platform	Platform	Platform	Platform
Exercise	Heavy Barbell Shrugs	Heavy Barbell Shrugs	Heavy Barbell Shrugs	Heavy Barbell Shrugs	Heavy Barbell Shrugs
Sets x Reps	4 x 8	4 x 8	4 x 8	4 x 8	4 x 8
AREA 3A	Dumbbell Racks	Dumbbell Racks	Dumbbell Racks	Dumbbell Racks	Dumbbell Racks
Exercise	Barbell / Dumbbell Upright Rows	Barbell / Dumbbell Upright Rows	Dumbbell Back Rows	Dumbbell Back Rows	Dumbbell Side Raise
Sets x Reps	2 x 8-10	2 x 8-10	2 x 8-10	2 x 8-10	2 x 8-10
AREA 3B	Machine Area	Dumbbell Racks	Dumbbell Racks		
Exercise	Dumbbell Side Raise	Dumbbell Rear Raise	Dumbbell Rear Raise		
Sets x Reps	2 x 8-10	2 x 8-10	2 x 8-10		
AREA 3B	Machine Area	Machine Area	Machine Area	Machine Area	
Exercise	Russian Twist	Triangle Crunch	Roller Stretch	Neck RT Side	
Sets x Reps	2 x 8-10	2 x 8-10	2 x 8-10	2 x 8-10	

IN-SEASON: GAME WEEKS					
MONDAY - LOWER BODY (ADD ROLLER)					
	Group 1 Students	Group 2 Students	Group 3 Students	Group 4 Students	Group 5 Students
AREA 1	Rack 1	Rack 2	Rack 3	Rack 4	Rack 5
Exercise	Barbell Squat	Barbell Squat	Barbell Squat	Barbell Squat	Barbell Squat

Sets x Reps	60% x 10 65% x 10 68% x 10 70% x 8	60% x 10 65% x 10 68% x 10 70% x 8	60% x 10 65% x 10 68% x 10 70% x 8	60% x 10 65% x 10 68% x 10 70% x 8	60% x 10 65% x 10 68% x 10 70% x 8
AREA 2	**Platform**	**Platform**	**Platform**	**Platform**	**Platform**
Exercise	Romanian Deadlifts	Romanian Deadlifts	Romanian Deadlifts	Romanian Deadlifts	Romanian Deadlifts
Sets x Reps	65% x 10 68% x 10 71% x 10 73% x 8	65% x 10 68% x 10 71% x 10 73% x 8	65% x 10 68% x 10 71% x 10 73% x 8	65% x 10 68% x 10 71% x 10 73% x 8	65% x 10 68% x 10 71% x 10 73% x 8
AREA 3A	**Dumbbell Racks**	**Dumbbell Racks**	**Dumbbell Racks**	**Dumbbell Racks**	**Dumbbell Racks**
Exercise	Barbell / Dumbbell Step Ups	Barbell / Dumbbell Step Ups	Barbell Lateral Lunge	Barbell Lateral Lunge	Barbell Lateral Lunge
Sets x Reps	2 x 8-10	2 x 8-10	2 x 8-10	2 x 8-10	2 x 8-10
AREA 3B	**Machine Area**	**Machine Area**	**Machine Area**	**Machine Area**	**Machine Area**
Exercise	Hamstring Curls	Leg Extensions	Roller Stretch	Front Plank Twist	Neck Back Push
Sets x Reps	2 x 8-10	2 x 8-10	2 x 8-10	2 x 8-10	2 x 8-10

IN-SEASON: GAME WEEKS					
WEDNESDAY - UPPER BODY (ADD ROLLER)					
	Group 1 Students	**Group 2 Students**	**Group 3 Students**	**Group 4 Students**	**Group 5 Students**
AREA 1	**Rack 1**	**Rack 2**	**Rack 3**	**Rack 4**	**Rack 5**
Exercise	Barbell Incline	Barbell Incline	Barbell Incline	Close-grip Bench Press	Close-grip Bench Press
Sets x Reps	60% x 10 65% x 10 70% x 8 70% x 8	60% x 10 65% x 10 70% x 8 70% x 8	60% x 10 65% x 10 70% x 8 70% x 8	4 x 8	4 x 8
AREA 1	**Rack 6 (Smith Machine)**				
Exercise	Close-grip Bench Press				
Sets x Reps	4 x 8				
AREA 2	**Platform**	**Platform**	**Platform**	**Platform**	**Platform**
Exercise	Heavy Barbell Shrugs	Heavy Barbell Shrugs	Heavy Barbell Shrugs	Heavy Barbell Shrugs	Heavy Barbell Shrugs
Sets x Reps	4 x 8	4 x 8	4 x 8	4 x 8	4 x 8
AREA 3A	**Dumbbell Racks**	**Dumbbell Racks**	**Dumbbell Racks**	**Dumbbell Racks**	**Dumbbell Racks**
Exercise	Barbell / Dumbbell Upright Rows	Barbell / Dumbbell Upright Rows	Dumbbell Back Rows	Dumbbell Back Rows	Dumbbell Side Raise
Sets x Reps	2 x 8-10	2 x 8-10	2 x 8-10	2 x 8-10	2 x 8-10
AREA 3B	**Machine Area**	**Dumbbell Racks**	**Dumbbell Racks**		
Exercise	Dumbbell Side Raise	Dumbbell Rear Raise	Dumbbell Rear Raise		
Sets x Reps	2 x 8-10	2 x 8-10	2 x 8-10		

AREA 3B	Machine Area	Machine Area	Machine Area	Machine Area	
Exercise	Russian Twist	Triangle Crunch	Roller Stretch	Neck RT Side	
Sets x Reps	2 x 8-10	2 x 8-10	2 x 8-10	2 x 8-10	

IN-SEASON: GAME WEEKS					
MONDAY - LOWER BODY (ADD ROLLER)					
	Group 1 Students	**Group 2 Students**	**Group 3 Students**	**Group 4 Students**	**Group 5 Students**
AREA 1	**Rack 1**	**Rack 2**	**Rack 3**	**Rack 4**	**Rack 5**
Exercise	Barbell Squat	Barbell Squat	Barbell Squat	Barbell Squat	Barbell Squat
Sets x Reps	60% x 10 63% x 10 67% x 10 67% x 10	60% x 10 63% x 10 67% x 10 67% x 10	60% x 10 63% x 10 67% x 10 67% x 10	60% x 10 63% x 10 67% x 10 67% x 10	60% x 10 63% x 10 67% x 10 67% x 10
AREA 2	**Platform**	**Platform**	**Platform**	**Platform**	**Platform**
Exercise	Romanian Deadlifts	Romanian Deadlifts	Romanian Deadlifts	Romanian Deadlifts	Romanian Deadlifts
Sets x Reps	63% x 10 67% x 10 70% x 10 73% x 10	63% x 10 67% x 10 70% x 10 73% x 10	63% x 10 67% x 10 70% x 10 73% x 10	63% x 10 67% x 10 70% x 10 73% x 10	63% x 10 67% x 10 70% x 10 73% x 10
AREA 3A	**Dumbbell Racks**	**Dumbbell Racks**	**Dumbbell Racks**	**Dumbbell Racks**	**Dumbbell Racks**
Exercise	Barbell / Dumbbell Step Ups	Barbell / Dumbbell Step Ups	Barbell Lateral Lunge	Barbell Lateral Lunge	Barbell Lateral Lunge
Sets x Reps	2 x 8-10	2 x 8-10	2 x 8-10	2 x 8-10	2 x 8-10
AREA 3B	**Machine Area**	**Machine Area**	**Machine Area**	**Machine Area**	**Machine Area**
Exercise	Hamstring Curls	Leg Extensions	Roller Stretch	Front Plank Twist or Side Planks	Neck Back Push
Sets x Reps	2 x 8-10	2 x 8-10	2 x 8-10	2 x 8-10	2 x 8-10

IN-SEASON: GAME WEEKS					
WEDNESDAY - UPPER BODY (ADD ROLLER)					
	Group 1 Students	**Group 2 Students**	**Group 3 Students**	**Group 4 Students**	**Group 5 Students**
AREA 1	**Rack 1**	**Rack 2**	**Rack 3**	**Rack 4**	**Rack 5**
Exercise	Barbell Incline	Barbell Incline	Barbell Incline	Close-grip Bench Press	Close-grip Bench Press
Sets x Reps	60% x 10 65% x 10 68% x 10 70% x 8	60% x 10 65% x 10 68% x 10 70% x 8	60% x 10 65% x 10 68% x 10 70% x 8	4 x 8	4 x 8
AREA 1	**Rack 6 (Smith Machine)**				
Exercise	Close-grip Bench Press				
Sets x Reps	4 x 8				
AREA 2	**Platform**	**Platform**	**Platform**	**Platform**	**Platform**
Exercise	Heavy Barbell Shrugs	Heavy Barbell Shrugs	Heavy Barbell Shrugs	Heavy Barbell Shrugs	Heavy Barbell Shrugs

Sets x Reps	3 x 10	3 x 10	3 x 10	3 x 10	3 x 10
AREA 3A	**Dumbbell Racks**	**Dumbbell Racks**	**Dumbbell Racks**	**Dumbbell Racks**	**Dumbbell Racks**
Exercise	Barbell / Dumbbell Upright Rows	Barbell / Dumbbell Upright Rows	Dumbbell Back Rows	Dumbbell Back Rows	Dumbbell Side Raise
Sets x Reps	2 x 8-10	2 x 8-10	2 x 8-10	2 x 8-10	2 x 8-10
AREA 3B	**Machine Area**	**Dumbbell Racks**	**Dumbbell Racks**		
Exercise	Dumbbell Side Raise	Dumbbell Rear Raise	Dumbbell Rear Raise		
Sets x Reps	2 x 8-10	2 x 8-10	2 x 8-10		
AREA 3B	**Machine Area**	**Machine Area**	**Machine Area**	**Machine Area**	
Exercise	Russian Twist	Triangle Crunch	Roller Stretch	Neck RT Side	
Sets x Reps	2 x 8-10	2 x 8-10	2 x 8-10	2 x 8-10	

IN-SEASON: GAME WEEKS					
MONDAY - LOWER BODY (ADD ROLLER)					
	Group 1 Students	**Group 2 Students**	**Group 3 Students**	**Group 4 Students**	**Group 5 Students**
AREA 1	**Rack 1**	**Rack 2**	**Rack 3**	**Rack 4**	**Rack 5**
Exercise	Barbell Squat	Barbell Squat	Barbell Squat	Barbell Squat	Barbell Squat
Sets x Reps	60% x 10 63% x 10 67% x 10	60% x 10 63% x 10 67% x 10	60% x 10 63% x 10 67% x 10	60% x 10 63% x 10 67% x 10	60% x 10 63% x 10 67% x 10
AREA 2	**Platform**	**Platform**	**Platform**	**Platform**	**Platform**
Exercise	Romanian Deadlifts	Romanian Deadlifts	Romanian Deadlifts	Romanian Deadlifts	Romanian Deadlifts
Sets x Reps	63% x 10 67% x 10 70% x 10	63% x 10 67% x 10 70% x 10	63% x 10 67% x 10 70% x 10	63% x 10 67% x 10 70% x 10	63% x 10 67% x 10 70% x 10
AREA 3A	**Dumbbell Racks**	**Dumbbell Racks**	**Dumbbell Racks**	**Dumbbell Racks**	**Dumbbell Racks**
Exercise	Barbell / Dumbbell Step Ups	Barbell / Dumbbell Step Ups	Barbell Lateral Lunge	Barbell Lateral Lunge	Barbell Lateral Lunge
Sets x Reps	2 x 8-10	2 x 8-10	2 x 8-10	2 x 8-10	2 x 8-10
AREA 3B	**Machine Area**	**Machine Area**	**Machine Area**	**Machine Area**	**Machine Area**
Exercise	Hamstring Curls	Leg Extensions	Roller Stretch	Front Plank Twist or Side Planks	Neck Back Push
Sets x Reps	2 x 8-10	2 x 8-10	2 x 8-10	2 x 8-10	2 x 8-10

IN-SEASON: GAME WEEKS					
WEDNESDAY - UPPER BODY (ADD ROLLER)					
	Group 1 Students	**Group 2 Students**	**Group 3 Students**	**Group 4 Students**	**Group 5 Students**
AREA 1	**Rack 1**	**Rack 2**	**Rack 3**	**Rack 4**	**Rack 5**
Exercise	Barbell Incline	Barbell Incline	Barbell Incline	Close-grip Bench Press	Close-grip Bench Press
Sets x Reps	60% x 10 63% x 10	60% x 10 63% x 10	60% x 10 63% x 10	3 x 10	3 x 10

	67% x 10 67% x 10	67% x 10 67% x 10	67% x 10 67% x 10		
AREA 1	**Rack 6 (Smith Machine)**				
Exercise	Close-grip Bench Press				
Sets x Reps	3 x 10				
AREA 2	**Platform**	**Platform**	**Platform**	**Platform**	**Platform**
Exercise	Heavy Barbell Shrugs	Heavy Barbell Shrugs	Heavy Barbell Shrugs	Heavy Barbell Shrugs	Heavy Barbell Shrugs
Sets x Reps	3 x 10	3 x 10	3 x 10	3 x 10	3 x 10
AREA 3A	**Dumbbell Racks**	**Dumbbell Racks**	**Dumbbell Racks**	**Dumbbell Racks**	**Dumbbell Racks**
Exercise	Barbell / Dumbbell Upright Rows	Barbell / Dumbbell Upright Rows	Dumbbell Back Rows	Dumbbell Back Rows	Dumbbell Side Raise
Sets x Reps	2 x 8-10	2 x 8-10	2 x 8-10	2 x 8-10	2 x 8-10
AREA 3B	**Machine Area**	**Dumbbell Racks**	**Dumbbell Racks**		
Exercise	Dumbbell Side Raise	Dumbbell Rear Raise	Dumbbell Rear Raise		
Sets x Reps	2 x 8-10	2 x 8-10	2 x 8-10		
AREA 3B	**Machine Area**	**Machine Area**	**Machine Area**	**Machine Area**	
Exercise	Russian Twist	Triangle Crunch	Roller Stretch	Neck RT Side	
Sets x Reps	2 x 8-10	2 x 8-10	2 x 8-10	2 x 8-10	

CROSS TRAINING FOR CONDITIONING

CROSS TRAINING COMBINATION EXERCISES #1

CROSS TRAINING COMBINATION EXERCISES #2

CROSS TRAINING COMBINATION EXERCISES #3

COOL DOWN STRETCHES

CONDITIONING: ASSIMULATING GAME TYPE TRAINING TO BUILD EDURANCE, EXPLOSION, & POWER
Dynamic Stretch: USED TO PREPARE BODY FOR POWER TYPE MOVEMENTS DURING COMPETITION
Conditioning Area 1
Conditioning Area 2 – Anaerobic Condition (80% - 90% run / 20-30% sec rest intervals
Conditioning Area 3 – TEAM BUILDING CONDITIONING

DRILLS FOR SPEED & QUICKNESS CHART

ACTIVITY	Speed Day
WARM-UP	WARM-UP
WARM-UP	WARM-UP

WEEKLY PRACTICE PLAN

Day of Week	Monday	Tuesday	Wednesday	Thursday	Friday	Saturday
Period / Time						
5 min						
5 min						
5 min						
5 min						
5 min						
5 min						
5 min						
5 min						
5 min						
5 min						
5 min						
5 min						
5 min						
5 min						
5 min						
5 min						
5 min						
5 min						
5 min						
5 min						
5 min						
5 min						
5 min						
5 min						
5 min						
5 min						
5 min						
5 min						
5 min						
5 min						

TEMPLATE: KINESIOLOGY TEST SCORECARD

KINESIOLOGY TEST SCORECARD (EXAMPLE) LOS ANGELES VALLEY COLLEGE PROFESSOR JAMES SIMS	NAME (LAST, FIRST, MIDDLE)	AGE: ____
	CIRCLE DAYS: M T W TH F Sa Su TIME:	NOTES / GOALS:
	KIN: ____ / LEVEL: 1 / 2 / 3 / 4	

TEST 1			TEST 2			TEST 3			TEST 4		
DATE 02/5/18	TOTAL POINTS 900		DATE	TOTAL POINTS		DATE	TOTAL POINTS		DATE	TOTAL POINTS	
CAL EQ NO# 2,797 calories per day	BODY COMP		CAL EQ NO#	BODY COMP		CAL EQ NO#	BODY COMP		CAL EQ NO#	BODY COMP	
	WEIGHT 227	BODY FAT% 17%		WEIGHT	BODY FAT%		WEIGHT	BODY FAT%		WEIGHT	BODY FAT%
PUSH UPS NO# 67	GRADE Excellent	PTS 100	PUSH UPS NO#	GRADE	PTS	PUSH UPS NO#	GRADE	PTS	PUSH UPS NO#	GRADE	PTS
V-UPS NO# 89	GRADE Above Ave	PTS 100	V-UPS NO#	GRADE	PTS	V-UPS NO#	GRADE	PTS	V-UPS NO#	GRADE	PTS
WT SQUAT NO# 25	GRADE Average	PTS 200	WT SQUAT NO#	GRADE	PTS	WT SQUAT NO#	GRADE	PTS	WT SQUAT NO#	GRADE	PTS
CARDIOVASCULAR EVENT: MILE RUN / JOG / WALK		PTS 200	CARDIOVASCULAR MILE RUN / JOG / WALK		PTS	CARDIOVASCULAR MILE RUN / JOG / WALK		PTS	CARDIOVASCULAR MILE RUN / JOG / WALK		PTS
TIME 10:21		PTS 25	TIME		PTS	TIME:		PTS	TIME:		
SIT & REACH INCHES NEG / POS = -3		PTS 25	SIT & REACH INCHES NEG / POS =		PTS	SIT & REACH INCHES NEG / POS =		PTS	SIT & REACH INCHES NEG / POS =		PTS
60 Secs VERTICAL PRESS 135 lbs. / 32x's		PTS 100	60 Secs VERTICAL PRESS		PTS	60 Secs VERTICAL PRESS		PTS	60 Secs VERTICAL PRESS		PTS
6 min STAIR RUN 18 rows completed		PTS 100	6 min STAIR RUN		PTS	6 min STAIR RUN		PTS	6 min STAIR RUN		PTS
60 Secs JUMP ROPE 52 ropes		PTS 50	60 Secs JUMP ROPE		PTS	60 Secs JUMP ROPE		PTS	60 Secs JUMP ROPE		PTS
EXTRA TEST IF NEEDED		PTS	EXTRA TEST IF NEEDED		PTS	EXTRA TEST IF NEEDED		PTS	EXTRA TEST IF NEEDED		PTS
		PTS			PTS	E		PTS			PTS
		PTS			PTS			PTS			PTS
		PTS			PTS			PTS			PTS

KINESIOLOGY CHARTS / FITNESS FOR LIFE

<table>
<tr><td colspan="2">KINESIOLOGY TEST SCORECARD

SCHOOL: _____

INSTRUCTOR: _____</td><td colspan="2">NAME (LAST,FIRST,MIDDLE)</td><td>AGE: ____</td></tr>
<tr><td></td><td></td><td colspan="2">CIRCLE DAYS: M T W TH F Sa Su
TIME:</td><td>NOTES / GOALS:</td></tr>
<tr><td></td><td></td><td colspan="3">KIN: _____ / LEVEL: 1 / 2 / 3 / 4</td></tr>
</table>

TEST 1			TEST 2			TEST 3			TEST 4		
DATE	TOTAL POINTS		DATE	TOTAL POINTS		DATE	TOTAL POINTS		DATE	TOTAL POINTS	
CAL EQ NO#	BODY COMP		CAL EQ NO#	BODY COMP		CAL EQ NO#.	BODY COMP		CAL EQ NO#	BODY COMP	
	WEIGHT	BODY FAT%		WEIGHT	BODY FAT%		WEIGHT	BODY FAT%		WEIGHT	BODY FAT%
PUSH UPS NO#	GRADE Excellent	PTS	PUSH UPS NO#	GRADE	PTS	PUSH UPS NO#	GRADE	PTS	PUSH UPS NO#	GRADE	PTS
V-UPS NO#	GRADE	PTS	V-UPS NO#	GRADE	PTS	V-UPS NO#	GRADE	PTS	V-UPS NO#	GRADE	PTS
WT SQUAT NO#	GRADE	PTS	WT SQUAT NO#	GRADE	PTS	WT SQUAT NO#	GRADE	PTS	WT SQUAT NO#	GRADE	PTS
CARDIOVASCULAR MILE RUN / JOG / WALK	GRADE		CARDIOVASCULAR MILE RUN / JOG / WALK	GRADE		CARDIOVASCULAR MILE RUN / JOG / WALK	GRADE		CARDIOVASCULAR MILE RUN / JOG / WALK	GRADE	
TIME: _____	PTS		TIME: _____	PTS		TIME: _____	PTS		TIME: _____	PTS	
SIT & REACH INCHES NEG / POS	PTS		SIT & REACH INCHES NEG / POS	PTS		SIT & REACH INCHES NEG / POS	PTS		SIT & REACH INCHES NEG / POS	PTS	
60 Secs VERTICAL PRESS	PTS		60 Secs VERTICAL PRESS	PTS		60 Secs VERTICAL PRESS	PTS		60 Secs VERTICAL PRESS	PTS	
6 min STAIR RUN	PTS		6 min STAIR RUN	PTS		6 min STAIR RUN	PTS		6 min STAIR RUN	PTS	
60 Secs JUMP ROPE	PTS		60 Secs JUMP ROPE	PTS		60 Secs JUMP ROPE	PTS		60 Secs JUMP ROPE	PTS	
	PTS			PTS		E	PTS			PTS	
	PTS			PTS			PTS			PTS	
	PTS			PTS			PTS			PTS	

122

EXAMPLE: MEN'S / WOMEN'S EXERCISE LOG-IN CARD FOR 2x's / WEEK

STUDENT NAME: _____

WEEK: _____

DAY# & DATE:				DAY# & DATE:		
CARDIOVASCULAR EXERCISE:				CARDIOVASCULAR EXERCISE:		
TIME / DISTANCE				TIME / DISTANCE		
DAY# 12 **LIFT NAME: POWER DAY**	**WEIGHT**	**SETS**	**REPS**	**PROGRAM SPECFICS**		
1. Flat Bench Press (BARBELL)	135,225, 315	3	12,10,5	Pyramid		
2. Flat Bench Press (cont.)	315,315, 225	3	5,5,10	Finished strong		
3. Military Press (BARBELL)	85,135,135,135	4	12,8,8,8	Power press		
4. Side lateral Raises (Dumbbell)	20's all sets	3	10 all	Body stationary		
5. Rear Deltoid machine	50,60,75	3	10 all	Back straight		
6. Deadlift (BARBELL)	135	2	12,12	Warm up		
7. Deadlift (BARBELL) cont.	225,275,315	3	10,8,6	Form concentrate		
8. Deadlift (BARBELL) cont.	405	3	5,5,5	Good form		
10. Machine Assisted Pull-ups	100	3	10 all	Form concentrate		
11. Front Back Pulley	100	4	10 all	Good form		
12. Seated Row Machine	80	3	10 all	Form concentrate		
13. Dumbbell Curls	35	3	10 all	Good form		
DAY# 13 **LIFT NAME: CIRCUIT DAY**	**WEIGHT**	**SETS**	**REPS**	**PROGRAM SPECFICS**		
1. Machine Leg Press	100,110,125	3	12	circuit all stations		
2. Hyperextension Machine	Body wt. only	3	12	circuit all stations		
3. Hamstring Curl Machine	20,25,30	3	12	circuit all stations		
4. One legged Extensions	30,40,50	3	12	circuit all stations		
5. Hammer Drive Machine	100, 125,125	3	12	circuit all stations		
6. Calf Raise Machine	65,75,85	3	12	circuit all stations		
7. Low Back Raise Machine	Body wt. only	3	12	circuit all stations		
8. Ab Crunch Machine	10,25,35	3	12	circuit all stations		
9. Right Side Planks	Body wt. only	3	12	circuit all stations		
10. Left Side Planks	Body wt. only	3	12	circuit all stations		
11. Regular Planks	Body wt. only	3	12	circuit all stations		
12. Abdominal Bicycle Crunches	Body wt. only	3	12	circuit all stations		
13. Push-ups (regular or modified)	Body wt. only	3	12	circuit all stations		

STUDENT NAME: _____

WEEK: _____

DAY# & DATE:				DAY# & DATE:			
CARDIOVASCULAR EXERCISE:				CARDIOVASCULAR EXERCISE:			
TIME / DISTANCE				TIME / DISTANCE			

DAY# LIFT NAME	WEIGHT	SETS	REPS	PROGRAM SPECFICS
1.				
2.				
3.				
4.				
5.				
6.				
7.				
8.				
10.				
11.				
12.				
13.				
14.				
15.				
DAY# LIFT NAME	WEIGHT	SETS	REPS	PROGRAM SPECFICS
1.				
2.				
3.				
4.				
5.				
6.				
7.				
8.				
9.				
10.				
11.				
12.				
13.				
14.				
15.				

STUDENT NAME: _____

WEEK: _____

DAY# & DATE:			DAY# & DATE:		
CARDIOVASCULAR EXERCISE:			CARDIOVASCULAR EXERCISE:		
TIME / DISTANCE			TIME / DISTANCE		
DAY# **LIFT NAME**	**WEIGHT**	**SETS**	**REPS**	**PROGRAM SPECFICS**	
1.					
2.					
3.					
4.					
5.					
6.					
7.					
8.					
10.					
11.					
12.					
13.					
14.					
15.					
DAY# **LIFT NAME**	**WEIGHT**	**SETS**	**REPS**	**PROGRAM SPECFICS**	
1.					
2.					
3.					
4.					
5.					
6.					
7.					
8.					
9.					
10.					
11.					
12.					
13.					
14.					
15.					

F.I.T.T. PRINCIPLE

F.I.T.T. PRINCIPLE EXERCISE CHECK SHEET					
DATE:				DAYS: M / T / W / R / F / S / Su	
NAME:					
Warm-up / Type	Frequency	Intensity	Time	Type	
Cardio					
Static Stretch					
Dynamic Stretch					
Ballistic Stretching					
Foam Roller Stretch					
Special Stretches					
Weight Exercises					
Type	Frequency	Intensity	Time	Type	Reps / Sets
Chest					/
Shoulders					/
Triceps					/
Back					/
Biceps					/
Quadriceps					/
Hamstrings					/
Abdominals					/
Calf's					/
Cardio-Exercise					
Type	Frequency	Intensity	Time	Type	
Power Walk					
Jog					
Running					
Cool Down	Frequency	Intensity	Time	Type	
Type					
Cardio					
Static Stretch					
Dynamic Stretch					
Ballistic Stretching					
Foam Roller Stretch					
Special Stretches					

CARDIOVASCULAR / MUSCULAR EDURANCE LOG – IN CARD

NAME: _____   TIME: _____

CARDIOVASCULAR / MUSCULAR EDURANCE		
DATE	TIME	EXERCISE PERFORMED

CARDIOVASCULAR / MUSCULAR EDURANCE		
DATE	TIME	EXERCISE PERFORMED

CARDIOVASCULAR / MUSCULAR EDURANCE		
DATE	TIME	EXERCISE PERFORMED

WEEKLY CARDIOVASCULAR FITNESS CHART: 4x's / WEEK

NAME:					WEEK OF:			
DATE	TIME	MONDAY ACTIVITY	DATE	TIME	TUESDAY ACTIVITY	DATE	TIME	WEDNESDAY ACTIVITY
DATE	TIME	THURSDAY ACTIVITY	DATE	TIME	FRIDAY ACTIVITY	DATE	TIME	WEEKEND ACTIVITY

RUBRIC CHART TEMPLATE

CLASS: DAY / TIME:

LAST NAME: _____

FIRST NAME: _____

RUBRIC SCALE DEFINED: A scoring rubric is an attempt to communicate expectations of quality around a task. Scoring rubrics are used to delineate consistent criteria for grading. Because the test is shared, a scoring rubric allows teachers and students to evaluate criteria. In addition, a scoring rubric can provide a basis for per review, reflection, and self – evaluation. It is aimed at fostering understanding, creating accurate and fair assessment, and can be an indication towards a way to proceed with subsequent learning and teaching. *Instructor: Use rubric scorecard below to place numbers in corresponding columns.*
SCORE = 1 = NO SKILLS, 2 = MARGINAL SKILLS, 3 = AVERAGE SKILLS, 4 = GOOD SKILLS, 5 = EXPECTIONAL SKILLS

	1 pt.	2 pts	3 pts	4 pts	5 pts
Pre- Cardio					
Exercise: 1 Mile Run	1				
Pre -Flexibility					
Exercise: Sit & Reach			3		
Pre-Circuit/Free Wt.					
Exercise: Machine Press		2			
				4	
Post-Cardio					
Exercise: 1 Mile Run			3		
Post-Flexibility					
Exercise: Sit & Reach					5
Post Circuit / Free Wt.					
Exercise: Machine Press			3		
					5
1. PRE-CLASS AVE					
2. POST-CLASS AVE					

RUBRIC CHART
ASSESSMENTS & MEASUREMENTS

CLASS: DAY / TIME:

LAST NAME: _____

FIRST NAME: _____

RUBRIC SCALE DEFINED: A scoring rubric is an attempt to communicate expectations of quality around a task. Scoring rubrics are used to delineate consistent criteria for grading. Because the test is shared, a scoring rubric allows teachers and students to evaluate criteria. In addition, a scoring rubric can provide a basis for per review, reflection, and self – evaluation. It is aimed at fostering understanding, creating accurate and fair assessment, and can be an indication towards a way to proceed with subsequent learning and teaching. *Instructor: Use rubric scorecard below to place numbers in corresponding columns.*
SCORE = 1 = NO SKILLS, 2 = MARGINAL SKILLS, 3 = AVERAGE SKILLS, 4 = GOOD SKILLS, 5 = EXPECTIONAL SKILLS

	1 pt.	2 pts	3 pts	4 pts	5 pts
Pre- Cardio					
Exercise: 1 Mile Run					
Pre -Flexibility					
Exercise: Sit & Reach					
Pre-Circuit/Free Wt.					
Exercise: Machine Press					
Post-Cardio					
Exercise: 1 Mile Run					
Post-Flexibility					
Exercise: Sit & Reach					
Post Circuit / Free Wt.					
Exercise: Machine Press					
1. PRE-CLASS AVE					
2. POST-CLASS AVE					

RUBRIC GRADE SCALE

I.   This numbered grade scale is used to measure and assess your improvements in physical fitness. Instructors can use the 3 standard exercises listed or add and subtract as desired. The definition of each number is located on the rubric card.

II. "Pre" assessments and measurements = testing at the beginning (1-2 weeks). "Post" assessments and measurements = the final testing during the last 1-2 weeks of the school term.

1 MILE RUN
*Measured in min/secs

5 = 7:30 & below	4 = 7:31- 9:00 min	3 =9:01- 10:30 min
2 = 10:31 - 12:00 min	1 = 12:01 & higher	

FLEXIBILITY/ SIT & REACH TEST
Measured in "inches

5 = +5 ½ - higher	4 = +5 - +1/2	3 = 0
2 = -1/2 - -5	1 = - 5 ½ or higher	

MACHINE PRESS TEST
60 sec / 1 minute: Women 35 lbs. / Men 85 lbs.

5 = 25x's or more	4 = 24 - 15x's	3 = 14 -10x's
2 = 9 - 5x's	1 = 4x's and below	

III. At the completion of the school term, gather all students to average pre and post scores. Add each individual number of each student, and then divide by how many students participated.

Example 1: "pre" class average = 104 total class score ÷ 40 total participating students = 2.6; this shows a below average/average skill level for class at the beginning of term (score 1-5 on rubric card).

Example 2: "post" class average = 178 total class score ÷ 40 total participating students = 4.45 (good /exceptional skills); this shows a major improvement during the class term (see score 1-5 on rubric card).

STATIC STRETCHES

NECK			
1. RT Lateral Stretch	**2. Rotating Stretch**	**3. Forward Flexion**	**4. Extension Stretch**

SHOULDER & BACK			
5. Parallel Arm Stretch	**6. Parallel Arm Stretch**	**7. Hug Shoulder Stretch**	**8. Bend Crossover Stretch**

SHOULDER & BACK	
9. Hands Behind Back Stretch	**10. Partner Hands Behind Back Stretch**

TRICEPS	FOREARMS	
11. Triceps Stretch	12. Kneel Forearm Stretch	13. Fingers Down Stretch

FOREARMS	
14. Finger-Wrist Stretch	15. Fingers Up Stretch

STOMACH	
16. Abdominal Stretch	17. Abdominal Stretch

LOWER BACK		
18. Seated Bent Back Stretch	**19. Seated Side Reach Stretch**	**20. Stand: Knee to Chest Stretch**

LOWER BACK	
21. Lying Down Double Knee-to Chest Stretch	**22. Lying Down Single Knee to Chest Stretch**

LOWER BACK		
23. Seated Reach Stretch	**24. Torso Twist**	**25. Lying Down Crossover Stretch**

LOWER BACK	
26. Lying Down Double Knee Over Stretch	**27. Lying Down Crossover Stretch**

LOWER BACK		
28. Seated Bent Knee Rotation Stretch	**29. Standing Side Bends**	**30. Seated Front Leg Tuck Stretch**

BUTTOCKS & HIPS		
31. Buddha Stretch	**32. Buddha Reach Forward Stretch**	**33. Pretzel Stretch**

BUTTOCKS & HIPS	
34. Twisting Glute Stretch	**35. Seated Ankle–to-Chest Stretch**

BUTTOCKS & HIPS	
36. Lying Quad Stretch	**37. Lying Side Quad Stretch**

HAMSTRINGS & ADDUCTORS		
38. Seated Quad Stretch	**39. Seated Reach Hamstring Stretch**	**40 Hamstring Stretch, RT, LF, Mid**

HAMSTRINGS & ADDUCTORS		
41. Seated Hamstring Stretch	**42. Seated Ankle/Hamstring Stretch**	**43. Lying Hamstring Stretch**

BUTTOCKS & HIPS	
44. Standing Reach Hamstring Stretch	**45. Standing Open Down (middle, RT, LF)**

BUTTOCKS & HIPS	
46. Standing Wide Grip Stretch	**47. Standing Hip Out**

CALVES & SHINS	
48. Standing Double Heels Up	**49. Standing Lean Back Stretch**

CALVES & SHINS	
50. Leaning Heel Down Stretch (wall assist)	**51. Double Ankle Sit (arms to feet)**

CALVES & SHINS	
52. Double Ankle Sit & reach	**53. Standing Bent Foot Stretch**

DYNAMIC STRETCHES: (use movement to accompany stretches: 2-3 steps forward, then stretch, return 2-3 steps backwards, then stretch (3-4 sets)

54. Dynamic: Power Kicks	55. Dynamic: Ankle Tuck Stretch	56. Dynamic: Heel to Toe Stretch

57. Dynamic: Lunge Hold Stretch	58. Dynamic: Lunge with a Twist	59. Dynamic: Bear in the Woods

STRENGTH MAX CHARTS: MEN & WOMEN

BENCH PRESS 1 REP MAX CHART									
MEN					WOMEN				
BODY WT	NOVICE	INTERMD	ADV	ELITE	BODY WT	NOVICE	INTERMD	ADV	ELITE
120	98	141	191	247	100	46	79	120	168
130	110	155	208	266	110	52	86	129	179
140	122	169	224	284	120	57	93	138	189
150	133	182	240	301	130	62	99	146	198
160	144	196	255	318	140	67	106	153	206
170	155	208	269	334	150	72	112	160	215
180	166	221	283	350	160	76	117	167	223
190	176	233	297	365	170	81	123	174	230
200	187	244	310	380	180	85	128	180	237
210	197	256	323	394	190	89	133	186	244
220	206	267	335	408	200	93	138	192	251
230	216	278	347	421	210	97	143	197	258
240	225	288	359	434	220	101	148	203	264
250	235	299	371	447	230	105	152	208	270
260	244	309	382	459	240	108	156	213	276
270	252	319	393	471	250	112	161	218	281
280	261	329	404	483	260	115	165	223	287
290	269	338	414	494					
300	278	347	425	506					
310	286	356	435	517					

SQUAT 1 REP MAX CHART									
MEN					WOMEN				
BODY WT	NOVICE	INTERMD	ADV	ELITE	BODY WT	NOVICE	INTERMD	ADV	ELITE
120	131	186	252	324	100	77	122	177	239
130	146	205	273	348	110	85	131	188	252
140	162	223	294	371	120	92	140	199	264
150	176	240	314	394	130	98	148	208	275
160	191	257	334	415	140	105	156	218	286
170	205	274	352	436	150	111	163	226	296
180	219	290	370	456	160	117	171	235	306
190	233	305	388	476	170	122	177	243	315
200	246	320	405	495	180	128	184	250	323
210	259	335	421	513	190	133	190	258	332
220	271	350	437	531	200	138	197	265	340
230	284	364	453	548	210	143	202	272	348
240	296	377	468	565	220	148	208	278	355
250	308	390	483	581	230	153	214	285	362
260	319	404	498	597	240	157	219	291	369
270	331	416	512	612	250	162	224	297	376
280	342	429	526	627	260	166	229	303	383
290	353	441	539	642					
300	363	453	552	656					

MILITARY PRESS 1 REP MAX CHART									
MEN					WOMEN				
BODY WT	NOVICE	INTERMD	ADV	ELITE	BODY WT	NOVICE	INTERMD	ADV	ELITE
120	63	94	131	172	100	35	57	84	114
130	71	103	142	184	110	38	61	89	120
140	79	113	153	197	120	42	65	94	126
150	86	121	163	208	130	45	69	98	131
160	93	130	173	219	140	48	72	102	136
170	100	138	182	230	150	50	76	107	141
180	107	146	192	240	160	53	79	110	145
190	114	154	200	250	170	56	82	114	149
200	120	162	209	260	180	58	85	118	153
210	127	169	218	269	190	60	88	121	157
220	133	176	226	279	200	63	91	124	161
230	139	183	234	287	210	65	94	127	165
240	145	190	242	296	220	67	96	130	168
250	151	197	249	304	230	69	99	133	171
260	157	204	256	313	240	71	101	136	175
270	162	210	264	320	250	73	104	139	178
280	168	216	271	328	260	75	106	142	181
290	173	222	278	336					
300	179	228	284	343					
310	184	234	291	350					

POWER CLEAN 1 REP MAX CHART									
MEN					WOMEN				
BODY WT	NOVICE	INTERMD	ADV	ELITE	BODY WT	NOVICE	INTERMD	ADV	ELITE
120	106	144	189	237	100	69	95	126	159
130	115	155	201	250	110	73	101	132	166
140	124	166	213	264	120	78	106	138	173
150	133	176	224	276	130	82	111	144	179
160	141	185	235	288	140	86	115	149	185
170	150	195	246	300	150	90	120	154	190
180	157	204	256	311	160	93	124	158	196
190	165	212	265	322	170	97	128	163	200
200	172	221	275	332	180	100	131	167	205
210	180	229	284	342	190	103	135	171	210
220	187	237	293	352	200	106	139	175	214
230	193	244	301	361	210	109	142	179	218
240	200	252	309	370	220	112	145	183	222
250	207	259	318	379	230	115	148	186	226
260	213	266	325	387	240	117	151	189	230
270	219	273	333	396	250	120	154	193	233
280	225	280	340	404	260	122	157	196	237
290	231	286	348	412					
300	237	293	355	419					

PULL UPS / BODY WEIGHT MAX CHART									
MEN					**WOMEN**				
BODY WT	**NOVICE**	**INTERMD**	**ADV**	**ELITE**	**BODY WT**	**NOVICE**	**INTERMD**	**ADV**	**ELITE**
120	7	15	26	38	100	< 1	6	14	23
130	7	15	26	37	110	< 1	7	14	22
140	7	15	25	36	120	< 1	7	13	21
150	7	15	25	35	130	< 1	6	13	20
160	7	14	24	34	140	< 1	6	12	20
170	7	14	23	33	150	< 1	6	12	19
180	7	14	22	32	160	< 1	6	11	18
190	7	13	22	31	170	< 1	6	11	17
200	6	13	21	30	180	< 1	5	10	16
210	6	12	20	29	190	< 1	5	10	16
220	6	12	20	28	200	< 1	5	9	15
230	6	11	19	27	210	< 1	4	9	14
240	6	11	18	26	220	< 1	4	9	14
250	5	11	18	25	230	< 1	3	8	13
260	5	10	17	24	240	< 1	3	8	12
270	5	10	17	24	250	< 1	3	7	12
280	4	10	16	23	260	< 1	2	7	11
290	4	9	15	22					
300	4	9	15	21					
310	4	9	14	21					

PUSH UPS / BODY WEIGHT MAX CHART									
MEN					**WOMEN**				
BODY WT	**NOVICE**	**INTERMD**	**ADV**	**ELITE**	**BODY WT**	**NOVICE**	**INTERMD**	**ADV**	**ELITE**
120	19	43	72	104	100	7	21	39	58
130	21	44	72	102	110	7	21	38	57
140	22	44	71	100	120	8	21	37	55
150	23	44	70	98	130	8	20	36	53
160	23	44	69	96	140	8	20	35	51
170	24	44	68	94	150	8	20	34	50
180	24	44	67	92	160	8	19	33	48
190	24	44	66	90	170	8	19	32	46
200	24	43	65	88	180	8	18	31	45
210	24	43	64	87	190	8	18	30	43
220	24	42	63	85	200	8	17	29	42
230	24	42	62	83	210	7	17	28	41
240	24	41	61	81	220	7	16	28	39
250	24	41	60	80	230	7	16	27	38
260	24	40	59	78	240	7	15	26	37
270	23	39	58	77	250	6	15	25	36
280	23	39	57	75	260	6	14	24	35
290	23	38	56	74					
300	23	38	55	73					

ABDOMINAL CRUNCHES / BODY WEIGHT MAX CHART

MEN BODY WT	NOVICE	INTERMD	ADV	ELITE	WOMEN BODY WT	NOVICE	INTERMD	ADV	ELITE
120	26	59	99	145	100	20	52	91	135
130	27	59	98	141	110	21	51	88	131
140	28	59	96	138	120	22	51	86	126
150	29	59	95	135	130	22	50	84	121
160	30	58	93	131	140	23	49	81	117
170	30	58	91	128	150	23	48	79	114
180	30	57	90	125	160	23	47	77	110
190	30	57	88	122	170	22	46	75	106
200	30	56	86	119	180	22	45	73	103
210	30	55	85	117	190	22	44	71	100
220	30	54	83	114	200	22	44	69	97
230	30	54	81	112	210	21	43	67	95
240	30	53	80	109	220	21	42	66	92
250	30	52	78	107	230	21	41	64	90
260	29	51	77	105	240	20	40	63	87
270	29	51	76	103	250	20	39	61	85
280	29	50	74	101	260	19	38	60	83
290	28	49	73	99					
300	28	48	72	97					
310	28	48	70	95					

*Remember to always consult with your physician before starting an exercise routine or nutrition plan. This will help create the best and safest results.